STRENGTH TRAINING FOR WOMEN

A Complete Guide to Strength Training for Every Woman at Every Stage

Mujahid Bakht

1

EBook ISBN: 979-8-89302-036-6

Paperback ISBN: 979-8-89302-037-3

Hardcover ISBN: 979-8-89302-038-0

Published by

Atlas Amazon, LLC.

United States of America

ABOUT THE AUTHOR

LIFE HISTORY: Mr. Bakhtis a mature, experienced, excessively enthusiastic, energetic administrator with thirty-eight years of proven experience as a businessman in international marketing and public relations. Mr. Bakht is an International Real Estate Specialist and Professional Business and Projects Consultant and Advisor. He was born in Pakistan and educated in Pakistan and the USA. Presently, American Citizen belongs to a business-oriented family. Thirty-eight years Resident of New York, USA.

BUSINESS HISTORY: Mr. Bakht is a Founder and President of Atlas Amazon, LLC., Mr. Bakht is a business developer and multilingual business specialist in the Caribbean, South East Asia, and the Middle East emerging markets Mr. Bakht has served, met, and hosted many heads of the States. Also, maintain a close relationship with investors of high net worth in the USA.

CAREER: Mr. Bakht has been engaged with many multinational companies in the fields of international real estate investment, communication, technology, diamond, gold, mining, Pre-Feb housing, wind and solar energy, outsourcing management, and project consulting, along with business partners and associates worldwide. Mr. Bakht has participated in major national and international conferences, including participated in United Nations (U.N.O.) conferences.

TRAVEL: Mr. Bakht is well-traveled and has visited many countries around the world.

MANAGEMENT EXPERIENCE: Thirty-eight years of diversified experience in project consulting, marketing, and business management. As a Director of Marketing, Director of Public Relations, Director of International Affairs, Executive Vice President, President, CEO, and Chairman of many national and multinational companies. Mr. Bakht hired and trained many professionals as business consultants in international marketing and supervised them.

CERTIFICATE OF ACHIEVEMENT: The Achievement Award was presented to Mr. Bakht by Stephen Fossler for five years of continued growth and customer satisfaction from 1996 to 2001.

HONORS MEMBER:Madison Who's Who of Professionals, having demonstrated exemplary achievement and distinguished contributions to the business community, registered at the Library of Congress in Washington D.C. USA. (2007 and 2008)

HONORS MEMBER: Premiere Who's Who International, professional business executive having demonstrated exemplary achievement and distinguished contributions to the International business community, 2008 and 2009.

CERTIFICATES: Certificate of Authenticity from Bill Rodham Clinton, President of the United States, and Hillary Rodham Clinton First Lady, USA. (July 20, 2000);

CERTIFICATE OF AUTHENTICITY: from Terence R. McAuliffe, Chairman of Democratic National Committee, Tom Dachle, Senate Democratic Leader, Dick Gephardt, House Democratic Leader, USA. (June 16, 2001);

CERTIFICATE OF AUTHENTICITY: from Terence R. McAuliffe, Chairman of Democratic National Committee, USA. (April 16, 2002).

TABLE OF CONTENTS

CHAPTER 1

Introduction to Strength Training

Strength training is not just about building muscle; it's a key part of staying healthy. Think of it as giving your body the tools to function at its best. When you lift weights or do body resistance exercises, you're doing more than just toning muscles—you're boosting your overall health in several significant ways.

Firstly, strength training increases muscle mass. This is important because muscles are crucial in burning calories, even when you're at rest. The more muscle you have, the more calories you burn throughout the day, which can help you maintain a healthy weight or lose fat.

But it's not all about weight. Strength training also strengthens bones. This is incredibly important, especially for women, as it can help reduce the risk of osteoporosis, a condition where bones become weak and fragile. By stressing bones, strength training increases bone density, making them stronger.

Moreover, regular strength training can help control blood sugar levels by improving how your body processes sugar. This can be particularly beneficial for people at risk of or managing diabetes. It improves insulin sensitivity, which helps maintain stable blood sugar levels.

Another great benefit is in how you feel every day. Strength training can boost your energy levels and improve your mood. The endorphins released during exercise can help you feel more energized and happier, fighting off feelings of depression and anxiety.

Building strength helps with everyday activities—carrying groceries, climbing stairs, or playing with kids becomes easier. It enhances your quality of life by improving your physical stamina and reducing fatigue.

Incorporating strength training into your fitness routine gives your body a fighting chance against common health issues, enhances your mood, and makes daily life easier and more enjoyable. So, why not grab those weights and give your health a lift?

Benefits specific to women

Strength training is often touted for enhancing muscle tone and endurance, but the benefits extend far beyond these general advantages for women. Engaging in regular strength training is a crucial part of maintaining health, especially as it offers several specific benefits that can significantly affect a woman's physical and mental wellness.

One of the primary reasons strength training is recommended for women is its effectiveness in aiding weight management. Muscle burns more calories than fat, so as women build muscle through strength training, they increase their basal metabolic rate, meaning they burn more calories even while at rest. This metabolic boost is particularly valuable as women age and naturally begin to lose muscle mass, which can slow down the metabolic rate and lead to weight gain. Women can counteract this decline by incorporating strength training into their routines, helping to maintain a healthier weight over time.

Moreover, strength training plays a vital role in cardiovascular health. Regular resistance training has been shown to lower blood pressure and improve cholesterol levels, which are key factors in preventing heart disease—a leading cause of death among women globally. Strength training helps safeguard against cardiovascular complications by strengthening the heart and improving blood circulation.

Another area where strength training significantly benefits women is the risk of osteoporosis. This bone-weakening condition is more prevalent in women than men, especially post-menopause, when declining estrogen levels reduce bone density. Strength training combats this by stressing the bones, which encourages the deposition of bone material and helps maintain bone thickness and strength. This is crucial for preventing osteoporosis and reducing the risk of fractures later in life.

Mental health benefits are also substantial. Strength training can alleviate symptoms of depression and anxiety by releasing endorphins, chemicals in the brain that act as natural painkillers and mood elevators. Additionally, achieving goals in strength training can boost confidence and self-esteem, further promoting mental well-being.

Strength training can be particularly beneficial for women undergoing menopause. It helps stabilize mood swings and decrease the severity of other menopausal symptoms like hot flashes and increased anxiety. Maintaining muscle mass during this period also aids in managing weight more effectively, which can become challenging due to hormonal changes that slow the metabolism.

Strength training proves valuable during and after pregnancy as well. It prepares the body for the physical demands of childbirth and can lead to a quicker postpartum recovery. Women who maintain a strength training program tailored to their needs during pregnancy often experience fewer complications and can return to their pre-pregnancy fitness levels sooner after giving birth.

Strength training improves insulin sensitivity and glucose metabolism, which is particularly important for women at risk of or managing type 2 diabetes. Strengthening the muscles, tendons, and ligaments around the joints can also help manage arthritis and other chronic conditions, alleviating joint stress and reducing pain.

Strength training is not just about enhancing physical appearance or building endurance; it's a comprehensive tool that supports long-term health and vitality. It offers women a way to protect against several health issues, boost metabolic health, strengthen bones, and enhance mental health, making it an essential component of a holistic approach to wellness. For women looking to improve their quality of life and ensure their health is supported through all stages of life, incorporating strength training into their regular exercise regimen is a powerful and effective strategy.

Common misconceptions about women and weightlifting

Many misconceptions discourage women from exploring the benefits of weightlifting, often fueled by outdated stereotypes or misinformation. Here's a closer look at some common myths and the truths that debunk them, presented in a straightforward and relatable manner.

Myth 1: Weightlifting Makes Women Bulky

A prevalent myth is that weightlifting automatically makes women bulky and overly muscular. This is far from the truth. Women generally have significantly lower testosterone levels than men, which is the hormone primarily responsible for increasing muscle size. Hence, gaining muscle mass is a slower and more controlled process for women. Most women who engage in regular strength training will see an increase in muscle tone and definition rather than bulk. The bulky bodybuilders often pictured in media are typically the result of intense, specific training regimens usually coupled with dietary strategies aimed at maximizing muscle gain.

Myth 2: Cardio Is Sufficient for Weight Loss; No Need for Weights

While cardiovascular exercises are practical for burning calories, strength training is equally essential for weight management and can be more efficient in the long run. Muscle tissue burns more calories than fat tissue, even when at rest. Women can boost their metabolism by increasing muscle mass through weightlifting, making it easier to maintain a healthy weight.

Additionally, unlike cardio alone, strength training ensures you lose fat without losing muscle, leading to a leaner, more toned appearance.

Myth 3: Women Should Only Lift Light Weights

There's a common belief that women should avoid heavy weights and stick to light ones to avoid getting too muscular. However, lifting heavier weights is essential for gaining strength and improving muscle tone. Light weights can only go so far in challenging your muscles; without adequate challenge, muscle growth and strength improvements are minimal. Women should aim to lift weights that are challenging for them personally, which will vary from one individual to another based on fitness levels and experience.

Myth 4: Weightlifting Is Dangerous for Women

Some believe that weightlifting is inherently risky and more likely to cause injury to women. In truth, when performed correctly and with proper technique, weightlifting is a safe exercise for both men and women. It strengthens bones and joints, reducing the risk of injuries in everyday activities. Starting with appropriate weights and possibly working with a trainer can help you learn the right form and progressively increase your lifting capacity safely.

Myth 5: Weightlifting Isn't Feminine

This myth stems from gender stereotypes that associate physical strength with masculinity. Strength and fitness, however, have no inherent gender, and weightlifting can benefit anyone, regardless of how they identify. The notion of femininity is subjective and culturally constructed, and many find strength to be a powerful expression of their femininity. Women who lift weights often report feeling more confident, empowered, and satisfied with their physical capabilities, which is a positive and affirming way to express self-regard, regardless of gender.

These misconceptions often deter women from engaging in or continuing weightlifting despite its numerous health benefits, including improved metabolism, increased bone density, and better cardiovascular health. Breaking down these myths encourages more women to start lifting and helps create a more inclusive and supportive fitness culture.

Overcoming barriers to start strength training

Starting strength training can be daunting, especially if you're new to the gym environment or have been inundated with conflicting information about the best approaches to building strength. Many people, particularly women, face various barriers when initiating a strength training routine. Understanding and finding ways to overcome these obstacles can pave the path to a successful and sustained lifting practice.

Lack of Knowledge

One of the most common barriers is simply not knowing where to start. The weightlifting world can seem overwhelming with different exercises, equipment, and techniques. Overcoming this requires a bit of education. Start small by learning the basics of fundamental exercises like squats, deadlifts, and bench presses. Plenty of resources are available, from online tutorials and fitness apps to books and personal trainers. Remember, every expert was once a beginner, and taking time to learn at your own pace is okay.

Intimidation and Gym Anxiety

It's common to feel intimidated the first few times you enter a gym, especially if you believe everyone else is more experienced or watching you. This feeling of gym anxiety is a significant hurdle for many. Consider starting your strength training at home with minimal equipment like dumbbells or resistance bands to combat this. As you gain confidence, you may feel more comfortable transitioning to a gym setting. Alternatively, going to the gym during off-peak hours when it's less crowded can ease you into the environment more gently.

Fear of Injury

Another barrier is the fear of getting hurt. The key to mitigating this fear is to focus on form and technique rather than lifting heavy weights immediately. Investing in a few sessions with a personal trainer who can guide you on proper form and help you set up a routine that fits your current fitness level and goals is beneficial. As you grow stronger and more confident in your movements, the fear of injury will likely diminish.

Time Constraints

Many people feel they can't fit strength training into their busy schedules. However, effective workouts don't necessarily have to be extended. Short, focused sessions of even 20 to 30 minutes can be efficient, mainly when performed consistently. Planning your workouts like any vital appointment can make them a non-negotiable part of your day.

Lack of Motivation

Sometimes, the most significant barrier is simply a lack of motivation. Setting clear, achievable goals can be a great motivator. Whether lifting a certain amount of weight, improving your overall health, or feeling better daily, having specific objectives can keep you focused. Tracking your progress through a fitness app or a traditional training log can provide a visible reminder of how far you've come and what you've accomplished, which can be incredibly motivating.

Cultural and Social Factors

Some women may feel that strength training is not for them because of cultural stereotypes or lack of representation in the fitness industry. Seeking out communities, either local or online, with like-minded individuals or groups that promote inclusivity in fitness can offer support and encouragement. Seeing others who share similar backgrounds or challenges thriving in strength training can inspire and reinforce the belief that you can do it, too.

Anyone can start and maintain a successful strength training regimen by acknowledging these barriers and actively seeking ways to overcome them. Remember, the benefits of lifting weights extend far beyond physical appearance, enhancing everything from bone density and metabolic health to psychological well-being. Taking the first steps might be challenging, but the long-term gains are worth the effort.

CHAPTER 2

The Female Physiology and Strength Training

Understanding the hormonal impact on strength training can significantly enhance your fitness journey, especially for women whose hormonal fluctuations are more pronounced due to menstrual cycles or menopausal changes. Hormones such as estrogen, Progesterone, testosterone, and cortisol play critical roles in how the body responds to and recovers from strength training.

Estrogen and Progesterone Estrogen and Progesterone are two primary hormones influencing women's bodies significantly. Estrogen, often considered the most dominant female hormone, helps to regulate the menstrual cycle and affects the musculoskeletal system. It promotes the healing of muscles and ligaments, which can benefit recovery from strength training. However, high levels of estrogen can also make connective tissues more lax, potentially increasing the risk of injuries during high-intensity workouts. This is particularly relevant during the ovulatory phase of a woman's cycle when estrogen peaks.

Conversely, Progesterone is known to increase catabolism, which is the breakdown of protein in the body. During the luteal phase of the menstrual cycle, when progesterone levels are higher, women may find it slightly more challenging to recover from muscle soreness. This phase can also bring about water retention, making some women feel bloated and less potent in their workouts.

While often considered a male hormone, testosterone is also present in women and plays a vital role in building muscle mass and strength. Women produce much smaller amounts, so muscle mass increases are more gradual in women than in men. However, the presence of testosterone means that women, too, can experience significant strength gains from resistance training. Understanding that these gains might be slower than their male counterparts can help set realistic expectations and patience.

Cortisol, the stress hormone, can profoundly impact how your body responds to strength training. In the short term, cortisol helps the body cope with exercise stress by breaking down fat and carbohydrates for energy. However, chronic high cortisol levels, possibly due to overtraining or insufficient recovery between workouts, can lead to muscle breakdown, poor performance, and a weakened immune system. Managing stress through adequate sleep, nutrition, and mindfulness or relaxation techniques is essential for keeping cortisol levels balanced.

Leveraging Hormonal Knowledge Knowing how these hormones fluctuate throughout the menstrual cycle can be a game changer in planning your training regimen. For instance, the follicular phase (from the start of menstruation to ovulation) often sees lower estrogen levels and Progesterone, potentially offering more optimal conditions for peak performance and strength training. During this phase, you focus on improving your lifts or trying new personal records.

In contrast, when hormone levels are higher and more fluctuant during the luteal phase, switching focus to maintenance, technique, or lighter, more endurance-based sessions might be beneficial. Recognizing these patterns and adapting your training accordingly can improve your results and make your strength training journey more comfortable and sustainable.

For women approaching or experiencing menopause, the decline in estrogen levels can affect bone density and muscle mass. Strength training becomes even more crucial at this stage to help mitigate bone loss and muscle atrophy, highlighting the importance of weight-bearing exercises.

Understanding the hormonal impacts on your body can enhance your approach to strength training. By aligning your workout intensity and type with your hormonal phases, you can optimize your physical performance and support your body's natural rhythms and needs, leading to more sustainable and effective fitness results.

Analyzing muscle fibre types and growth potential

Muscle fibres in the human body can be broadly categorized into two types: Type I, known as slow-twitch fibres, and Type II, known as fast-twitch fibres. Each type has unique characteristics and plays different roles in physical activities and strength training, affecting how muscles respond to exercise and their growth potential.

Type I muscle fibres are highly efficient at using oxygen to generate more fuel (ATP) for continuous, extended muscle contractions. They are slower to fire than fast-twitch fibres but can sustain activity for longer without fatigue. This makes them ideal for endurance activities such as long-distance running or cycling. While they don't increase in size as dramatically as fast-twitch fibres, they can improve efficiency and stamina through appropriate training.

On the other hand, Type II muscle fibres excel in producing quick, powerful bursts of speed or strength. These fibres fatigue faster but are crucial for activities that require force and speed, such as sprinting or lifting heavy weights. Due to their nature, Type II fibers have a higher potential for growth in size and strength, which is particularly significant for those engaged in strength training.

The ratio of slow-twitch to fast-twitch fibers varies from person to person and is primarily determined by genetics. This ratio can influence what types of physical activities each individual might excel at naturally. However, it's important to note that targeted training can enhance the efficiency or performance of both types of fibers beyond their natural predispositions.

Training should focus on prolonged, low—to moderate-intensity endurance exercises to enhance the performance and endurance of Type I fibers. This activity helps these fibers become more capable of utilizing oxygen efficiently, thus improving stamina and endurance over time. Conversely, to maximize the growth potential of Type II fibers, incorporating high-intensity training that includes weight lifting or explosive movements is crucial. This kind of training stimulates these fibers to grow in size and enhance strength, making them essential for those looking to increase muscle mass and power.

When designing strength training routines, it is beneficial to consider both types of muscle fibers. Focusing on exercises that promote fast and forceful muscle contractions with adequate rest periods can lead to significant gains for those aiming to increase muscle size and strength. These activities target the fast-twitch fibers, encouraging their growth and development. Meanwhile, integrating some endurance training can help improve the efficiency of slow-twitch fibers, which supports overall fitness and health, providing a balanced approach to physical conditioning.

Understanding the differences between these muscle fibers and how they respond to various forms of exercise can help individuals tailor their fitness routines to suit their goals better. Whether aiming for strength, endurance, or a combination, leveraging this knowledge can lead to more effective training outcomes, helping individuals optimize their workouts for maximum benefit and efficiency. This personalized fitness approach caters to individual strengths and weaknesses and promotes long-term health and performance enhancements.

Training around the menstrual cycle

Training around the menstrual cycle is a thoughtful approach that can optimize a woman's strength training results by aligning workout intensity with the hormonal fluctuations throughout the cycle. Understanding how the menstrual cycle affects energy levels, strength, and recovery can help tailor exercise routines to be more effective and comfortable.

The menstrual cycle is typically divided into four phases: menstrual, follicular, ovulation, and luteal. Each phase has unique changes in hormone levels, particularly estrogen and Progesterone, which can influence a woman's strength and energy levels.

During the **menstrual phase**, which is the start of the cycle marked by menstruation, many women experience lower energy levels and some discomfort due to cramps and other symptoms. It's often a good time to engage in lighter, less intense workouts. Activities like yoga, light cardio, or gentle strength training can be beneficial during this time, helping to manage discomfort without overstraining the body.

As the cycle progresses into the **follicular phase**, which follows menstruation and leads to ovulation, estrogen levels rise. This increase in estrogen tends to boost energy levels, mood, and pain tolerance. These factors can make it an excellent time for more intense and heavy strength training. Women might perform better, lift heavier, and recover quicker during this phase.

Ovulation marks the midpoint of the cycle, where estrogen peaks just before ovulation and begins to drop afterward, while Progesterone starts to rise. The peak in estrogen can lead to maximum strength and performance, making it a good time to attempt personal bests or engage in high-intensity workouts. However, some women might also experience joint laxity due to hormonal fluctuations, so it's essential to be cautious and avoid injury by ensuring proper form and technique.

The **luteal phase** follows ovulation and leads up to menstruation. During this phase, rising progesterone levels can increase the body's temperature and potentially affect heart rate. Some women may feel more fatigued, less coordinated, and less able to perform at peak levels. This is a time to focus on moderate activities and maintain consistency rather than push for performance peaks. It can also be a reasonable period for incorporating more recovery-focused practices, such as stretching and mobility work, to aid muscle recovery and prepare for the next cycle.

Being aware of and responsive to these changes throughout the menstrual cycle, women can plan their training schedule more effectively. This approach enhances performance and aligns training with the body's natural rhythms, potentially reducing the risk of injury and improving overall training outcomes. It's also crucial to remember that every woman's experience with her menstrual cycle is unique. Keeping a training diary that tracks the phases of the cycle alongside workout details can be a practical method for understanding personal patterns and adjusting training plans accordingly. This personalized approach helps create a fitness regimen that respects and adapts to the physiological states throughout the menstrual cycle, promoting better health and fitness achievements.

Age-related physiological changes and their implications

As women age, their bodies undergo various physiological changes that can significantly affect strength training. Understanding these changes can help adapt fitness routines to ensure continued effectiveness while minimizing the risk of injury.

One of the most prominent changes is the decrease in estrogen levels, particularly evident during and after menopause. Estrogen plays a crucial role in maintaining bone density and strength. With its decline, women become more susceptible to osteoporosis and bone fractures. This loss of bone density underscores the importance of weight-bearing exercises in fitness routines. Strength training, in particular, can help counteract bone loss by stimulating bone formation and slowing deterioration. Regular resistance training helps maintain bone health and enhances muscle mass and strength, which naturally decline with age.

Muscle mass also tends to decrease as part of the natural aging process, a condition known as sarcopenia. This reduction in muscle mass can lead to decreased metabolic rate, weight gain, and reduced physical capacity, which can affect daily activities and overall quality of life. However, strength training can significantly mitigate these effects by preserving and even increasing muscle fiber size and strength. Regular strength training exercises help maintain muscle functionality, enhance metabolic health, and support independence in later life.

Another change that occurs with aging is the reduction in joint flexibility and range of motion. This can be attributed to various factors, including the loss of elasticity in tendons and ligaments and the development of joint conditions such as arthritis. It is beneficial to include flexibility and mobility exercises as part of a regular workout regimen to address these issues. Practices such as yoga or dynamic stretching can complement strength training by improving flexibility, reducing stiffness, and alleviating joint pain.

As the body ages, the recovery process from physical activities tends to lengthen, and the risk of injuries increases. Therefore, focusing on proper technique and gradual progression in workouts becomes crucial. Older adults should ensure adequate recovery time between strenuous sessions to prevent overtraining and stress injuries. A balanced routine that includes adequate rest, proper hydration, and nutrition supports recovery and overall health.

Cardiovascular health can also decline with age, making aerobic exercise an essential component of a fitness regimen for older women. Regular cardiovascular activity, such as brisk walking, cycling, or swimming, can help improve heart health, increase stamina, and maintain endurance. Combining cardiovascular exercises with strength training creates a comprehensive fitness program that addresses various health aspects, helping maintain vitality and functional ability as women age.

By adjusting training strategies to accommodate these age-related physiological changes, older women can continue to reap the benefits of an active lifestyle. Strength training, flexibility, and aerobic exercises play a critical role in managing the challenges of aging. They help maintain physical health and boost psychological well-being, enhancing quality of life in the later years.

CHAPTER 3

Setting Clear Goals

Setting clear goals is fundamental to any successful strength training program, especially for women looking to maximize their fitness outcomes. Whether you're new to lifting weights or a seasoned athlete, defining your goal sets a direction and provides motivation. This chapter will guide you through establishing clear, achievable goals and how these objectives can be strategically aligned with your fitness journey. We'll explore how to set goals that are not only ambitious but also tailored to your unique needs, lifestyle, and your body's natural capabilities. By the end of this chapter, you'll understand how to craft a roadmap that empowers you to progress steadily toward your desired fitness outcomes, keeping you engaged and motivated every step of the way.

Differentiating between aesthetic, health, and performance goals

Differentiating between aesthetic, health, and performance goals is essential for tailoring your strength training program to meet specific needs and expectations. Each type of goal focuses on different outcomes, and understanding these can help you prioritize your efforts and select the right exercises and routines.

Aesthetic goals are centered on changing the physical appearance of your body. Many people engage in strength training to enhance their muscle definition, reduce body fat, and achieve a more sculpted physique. Training for aesthetic goals typically involves resistance training to build muscle and cardiovascular exercises to reduce fat. The key is maintaining a balanced diet and workout regimen targeting various muscle groups to achieve a proportionate and toned body.

Health-related goals focus on improving overall well-being and bodily functions. This could include increasing bone density, enhancing cardiovascular health, reducing the risk of chronic diseases such as diabetes or hypertension, or improving metabolic efficiency. Strength training for health purposes doesn't necessarily aim to alter one's appearance but to promote longevity and reduce the incidence of illness and injury. Workouts toward health goals often emphasize full-body fitness, incorporate moderate-intensity activities, and prioritize consistency and sustainability over intensity.

Performance goals enhance your ability to perform a specific task or activity. This could be improving your strength to lift a certain amount of weight, increasing your endurance to perform several repetitions of a particular exercise, or enhancing your overall athletic capabilities for sports. Performance training involves focusing on specific skills and progressively increasing the intensity and complexity of workouts to push the limits of what your body can do. Regular practice, training, and adequate rest and recovery are required to prevent overtraining and injuries.

Each type of goal requires a different approach to training and nutrition and variations in intensity, volume, and progression. Understanding the nuances between aesthetic, health, and performance goals allows you to create a more effective and targeted workout plan. This distinction also helps set realistic expectations and measure progress according to the proper criteria, ensuring you remain motivated and advance in your fitness journey.

Importance of setting SMART goals

The importance of setting SMART goals in strength training cannot be overstated. SMART, an acronym for Specific, Measurable, Achievable, Relevant, and Time-bound provides a framework that helps ensure your fitness goals are clear and attainable. This approach not only enhances motivation but also increases the likelihood of achieving the desired outcomes.

Specific goals provide a clear direction. Instead of setting a vague goal like "get fit," specify what "fit" means. It could be "increase my bench press weight by 20 pounds" or "run a 5k without stopping." Specificity helps focus your efforts and makes it easier to plan your training sessions.

Measurable goals allow for tracking progress. By quantifying your goals, such as setting a target weight for lifting or a specific body fat percentage to reach, you can periodically assess how close you are to achieving them. This provides motivation as you see tangible progress and helps you adjust your training regimen if you are not on track.

Achievable goals ensure you set targets within reach, considering your current fitness levels and resources. While it's good to be ambitious, setting goals that are too challenging can lead to frustration and decrease your motivation. Achievable goals challenge you but are within your capacity to attain with effort.

Relevant goals align with your more considerable fitness and lifestyle aspirations. If you're training for a marathon, focusing primarily on upper-body strength might not be appropriate. Your goals should contribute towards broader objectives, whether health, aesthetics, or performance, ensuring that your efforts are focused and coherent.

Time-bound goals impose a deadline, creating a sense of urgency that can spur action. Whether you're aiming to lift a certain weight in three months or preparing for a competition by the end of the year, having a timeframe helps you organize your training phases, measure progress, and stay committed.

Using the SMART criteria, you create a structured and thoughtful approach to setting goals tailored to your personal fitness journey. This methodical approach helps maintain motivation by providing clear milestones and deadlines. It enhances the effectiveness of your training by ensuring that your goals are realistic and aligned with your fitness needs and lifestyle.

Adjusting goals based on lifestyle and baseline fitness

Adjusting your goals based on lifestyle and baseline fitness is crucial for creating a sustainable strength training program that integrates seamlessly into your daily routine and reflects your current physical condition. This personalized approach ensures that your fitness objectives are practical and achievable, reducing the risk of burnout or injury.

Consider Lifestyle Factors Your lifestyle plays a significant role in shaping your fitness goals. Factors such as work commitments, family responsibilities, and social activities all influence the amount of time and energy you can dedicate to training. For instance, if you have a demanding job or young children, setting a goal to train for two hours daily might be unrealistic. Instead, you might aim for shorter, more intense sessions a few times a week or even 30-minute workouts that can be easily accommodated into your schedule.

Consider your access to facilities and equipment. If you don't have a gym membership or home equipment, your goals might need to focus on bodyweight exercises or routines that require minimal equipment. This adaptation ensures that your goals are attainable within your current circumstances.

Assess Baseline Fitness Your current fitness level also determines your goals' appropriateness. Those just starting out should focus on building foundational strength and endurance, with goals that gradually increase in difficulty. For example, a beginner might aim to complete a full set of bodyweight exercises before progressing to adding weights.

Conversely, if you are already an experienced exerciser, your goals might be more about refining techniques, increasing weights, or enhancing performance. The key is to set goals that challenge you without exceeding your physical limits, which can lead to overtraining and injury.

Dynamic Goal Adjustment Fitness is a dynamic process, and your goals should evolve as your lifestyle and fitness levels change. Regularly reassessing your goals ensures they align with your life's realities and physical progress. This might mean scaling back if you're going through a particularly stressful period or stepping up your goals as your fitness improves.

It's also beneficial to have flexible sub-goals that can be adjusted quickly. For example, instead of a rigid goal of losing 10 pounds in a month, consider a range of losing 8-10 pounds, or focus on reducing body fat percentage instead of just weight. This flexibility can help maintain motivation and accommodate changes in your circumstances without feeling like you're falling short.

Ultimately, aligning your goals with your lifestyle and baseline fitness makes your objectives more attainable and helps integrate fitness into your life as a permanent and enjoyable part of your routine. Recognizing and respecting your personal context creates a balanced approach to strength training that fosters physical and mental well-being.

Regularly reviewing and updating your goals

Regularly reviewing and updating your goals is crucial to maintaining a successful strength training program. This continuous process ensures that your fitness objectives align with your evolving abilities and interests, helping you stay motivated and on track.

When you set initial goals for your strength training, these serve as benchmarks to measure your progress. However, your physical and mental states change as you engage in regular workouts. What once seemed challenging may become more manageable, or you may encounter unexpected hurdles that make some goals less attainable. By scheduling regular reviews—perhaps monthly or at the end of a training cycle—you can assess how well your current goals match your progress and personal satisfaction.

During these evaluations, it's important to consider your achievements and any difficulties you've faced. If you surpass your current goals more quickly than anticipated, this might involve adjusting your targets upward. On the other hand, if you're consistently falling short, it might be necessary to set more realistic goals that still push your limits but are within reach. This balance prevents frustration and keeps you motivated.

Your interests and priorities might shift as you progress in your fitness journey. You may have begun with a focus on weight loss but have grown to appreciate the strength and endurance benefits of your workouts. Regularly updating your goals allows you to incorporate these new insights and interests into your regimen, which keeps your routine fresh and engaging.

Feedback is another critical component of this process. Reflecting on what aspects of your routine are working well and which aren't can provide valuable insights that help refine your approach. For example, you might discover that specific exercises are practical or enjoyable, prompting you to focus more on these in your plan. Conversely, you may phase out activities that aren't delivering value or enjoyment.

Additionally, the feedback you receive from others, such as trainers or workout partners, can offer a different perspective that helps further fine-tune your training approach. They might notice things you don't and provide improvement tips you hadn't considered.

The process of achieving and setting new goals can be incredibly motivating. Meeting smaller, incremental objectives gives you a sense of accomplishment and propels you towards more extensive, long-term aims. This feeling of progress is essential for staying engaged and committed to your strength training program.

Regularly reviewing and adjusting your goals is fundamental to a dynamic and effective strength training strategy. It ensures that your fitness activities remain challenging, enjoyable, and closely tailored to your growth and changing needs, ultimately enhancing both your results and enjoyment of the journey.

CHAPTER 4

Essential Equipment and Gym Familiarity

Starting a strength training routine involves more than determination and a workout plan; it also means knowing the right equipment and how to use it effectively. In this chapter, we'll introduce you to the crucial equipment you'll find in a gym or might consider adding to your home gym setup. We will explore different types of equipment, such as free weights and machines, detailing their uses and how they can benefit your training. Additionally, we'll offer practical advice on becoming comfortable and confident in your workout environment, whether at home or in a commercial gym. Knowing how to use this equipment properly will improve the quality of your workouts, help you avoid injuries, and get the most out of your fitness journey.

Choosing between a home gym and a commercial gym

Choosing between setting up a home gym and joining a commercial gym involves weighing various factors to determine which option best suits your lifestyle, fitness goals, and budget.

Convenience and Accessibility A home gym offers unparalleled convenience. There's no travel time, and you can work out any time that fits your schedule, making it easier to stay consistent with your training. This can be particularly appealing if you have a busy schedule or are uncomfortable working out in public spaces. However, the initial setup of a home gym requires space and a significant upfront investment in equipment.

On the other hand, a commercial gym might be less convenient regarding travel and operating hours but usually offers a broader range of equipment than most people can feasibly fit or afford in their home setup. This variety can be crucial for a well-rounded strength training regimen and provide more versatility in your workouts.

Cost Considerations Financially, the decision varies based on long-term vs. short-term investment. Home gyms require purchasing equipment, which might seem costly upfront but eliminates ongoing membership fees. Depending on the equipment quality and your fitness requirements, setting up a home gym could range from a modest to a substantial financial outlay. Conversely, commercial gyms charge monthly or yearly fees, which spreads the cost over time and often includes access to high-end equipment, classes, and other facilities.

Social Environment Commercial gyms offer a social environment that can motivate many people. Working out around others can increase motivation and commitment to a fitness routine. Gyms may also provide access to professional trainers who can offer guidance, help perfect your technique, and keep you accountable. A commercial gym might be the better choice for those who thrive in a community setting.

Space and Equipment Quality If you prefer specific types of equipment, such as high-end treadmills, specialized weight machines, or swimming pools, a commercial gym is likely your best bet. Home gyms are limited by the space available and the practicality of certain pieces of equipment. However, a home gym is more convenient if you're focused on weightlifting or essential cardio.

Personal Comfort and Hygiene A home gym offers privacy and hygiene that a public gym can't match. At home, you don't have to wait for equipment to become available; you know who has used it and how it's been cleaned. A home gym is safer and more comfortable for those concerned about germs, especially during flu season or a pandemic.

Flexibility and Freedom A home gym allows you to work out however and whenever you want. There's no need to worry about gym rules, opening hours, or the etiquette of sharing equipment. You can play your music, wear whatever you want, and design a workout space you enjoy.

Choosing between a home gym and a commercial gym depends on your specific needs and preferences. Consider your budget, space, fitness goals, social preferences, and lifestyle to make the best decision for your fitness journey.

Essential equipment for home-based strength training

When setting up a home gym for strength training, choosing the right equipment is crucial to ensure you can perform a variety of effective workouts without needing to invest in a lot of space or expensive machinery. The essential pieces you select should allow versatility and scalability in your fitness routine.

Firstly, adjustable dumbbells can be a cornerstone of any home gym. These are particularly space-efficient and cost-effective, as they replace the need for multiple sets of weights. Adjustable dumbbells can be used for various exercises, from basic curls and tricep extensions to more complex moves like dumbbell presses and rows.

Another key piece of equipment is a sturdy bench. A good-quality bench provides the foundation for numerous exercises and should ideally be adjustable to allow for incline and decline variations. This enhances the range of exercises you can perform, including bench presses, dumbbell rows, and even certain types of leg workouts.

Resistance bands are also invaluable for a home gym. These are not only affordable and space-saving but also remarkably versatile. Resistance bands can add difficulty to bodyweight exercises, assist strength training, and even mimic many cable machine exercises.

For those looking to incorporate cardio into their strength training routine, a jump rope or a compact cardio machine like a stationary bike or a rowing machine might be worthwhile additions. These can help warm your body before strength sessions and provide a quick, effective way to burn calories and improve cardiovascular health.

A yoga mat and a foam roller can be essential for warm-ups, cool-downs, and recovery days. A mat provides a comfortable surface for stretching and core workouts, while a foam roller can be used for self-myofascial release, helping to relieve muscle tightness and improve blood flow.

You can create a versatile and effective home gym that supports a wide range of strength training exercises by selecting these essential items. This will help you achieve your fitness goals without the need for a large space or a significant financial investment. With the right setup, you can maintain a comprehensive strength training regimen from the comfort of your own home.

Getting familiar with gym equipment

Getting familiar with gym equipment is crucial for anyone looking to enhance their workout effectiveness and ensure safety during exercise. Whether you're new to the gym scene or returning after a break, understanding how to use different pieces of equipment can significantly boost your confidence and performance.

It's beneficial to start with the basics, starting with the most commonly used pieces of equipment in most gyms: free weights, such as dumbbells and barbells. These allow for a range of exercises that can target almost every muscle group in the body. Familiarizing yourself with different weight sizes and learning the correct form for basic lifts like bicep curls, bench presses, and squats can lay a solid foundation for your training.

Resistance machines are also a staple in many gyms and are particularly useful for beginners because they help guide your movements and reduce the risk of injury. Each machine typically targets a specific muscle group, which can be very effective for strength training routines focused on muscle isolation. Adjust the seat and weight settings to match your height and strength level, ensuring each movement feels comfortable and practical.

Another important category of gym equipment includes cardiovascular machines such as treadmills, elliptical trainers, stationary bikes, and rowing machines. These machines are relatively straightforward and designed to help improve cardiovascular health. However, it's important to adjust the settings to suit your fitness levels, such as the speed on a treadmill or the resistance on a bike, to avoid overexertion.

Functional fitness equipment like kettlebells, medicine balls, and sandbags offers versatility and can be used for various exercises that improve strength, balance, and coordination. Engaging with these tools often involves more complex movements like kettlebell swings or medicine ball slams, so proper instruction on form and technique is beneficial to maximize the benefits and minimize the risk of injury.

For those who enjoy a structured workout, cable machines are a great way to perform various exercises with adjustable resistance. These machines use a system of pulleys and weights to provide resistance and can be adjusted to perform exercises for both the upper and lower body. Understanding how to modify the attachments and adjust the resistance can allow for a highly customizable workout.

Don't overlook the importance of safety and hygiene when using gym equipment. Always check that the equipment is in good working order before use and clean the machine before and after your workout to help maintain a hygienic environment.

If you're unsure how to use any equipment, don't hesitate to ask a gym staff member or personal trainer for assistance. Most gyms offer an introductory session to new members to walk them through the various types of equipment available. Taking advantage of this can be a great way to ensure you're using the equipment correctly and safely, maximizing your workout results while minimizing the risk of injury.

Safety tips for using gym equipment

Using gym equipment safely prevents injuries and ensures an effective workout. Here are several safety tips that can help you navigate using gym equipment effectively and securely.

Before you start using any gym equipment, it's essential to warm up your muscles. A light cardio session or dynamic stretching can increase blood flow to the muscles and decrease the risk of strains and sprains. This prepares your body for the physical stress of weight lifting or resistance training.

Always take a moment to read the instructions on any new equipment you plan to use, even if you have been exercising for years. Most gym machines come with diagrams and step-by-step instructions on properly operating them. Familiarizing yourself with these can prevent misuse and injuries.

Ensure your equipment is adjusted to fit your body size and strength level. This includes changing the seat height, the position of safety bars, and the weights you lift. Using equipment that isn't adjusted correctly can lead to improper form, which might cause injuries. For instance, a weight bench that's too high or too low can strain your back or neck during lifts.

Always prioritize proper form over lifting heavier weights or performing exercises faster. Incorrect form, especially under heavy loads, can quickly lead to injuries. If you're unsure about your form, ask a trainer for a demonstration or tips. Trainers can provide immediate feedback and corrections that significantly reduce your risk of getting hurt.

Staying focused on the exercise you are performing while using gym equipment is crucial. Distractions can lead to improper form or forgetting to engage safety mechanisms, which increases the risk of injury. For example, not paying attention while setting down weights can lead to crushed fingers or toes or, worse, dropping weights on yourself or others.

It's essential to move through your exercises at a controlled pace. Rushing through your workout compromises your form and safety. Quick, jerky movements are more likely to lead to muscle pulls or accidents with the equipment. Instead, focus on controlled, smooth motions that ensure you use your muscles effectively and safely.

Following these tips can help you enjoy a safe and productive gym experience. Remember that consistency and attention to safety are just as important as pushing your limits in strength training.

CHAPTER 5

Core Strength Training Principles

In any effective strength training program, understanding and applying core principles are key to achieving optimal results and maintaining safety. This chapter delves into the foundational concepts that govern practical strength training, including progressive overload, the importance of rest and recovery, and the balance between volume and intensity. These principles form the bedrock of all successful strength training routines, helping you maximize gains, prevent injuries, and ensure long-term progress. By mastering these essential elements, you'll be able to create a training regimen that challenges you, adapts to your growing capabilities, and helps you reach your fitness goals efficiently.

Progressive overload

Understanding progressive overload is essential to continually improving your strength and fitness. Essentially, progressive overload means gradually increasing the amount of stress you place on your body during training. This concept is the cornerstone of practical strength training because it helps ensure your muscles adapt and grow stronger over time.

Think of it this way: when you challenge your muscles by pushing them a little harder each time, you're sending a signal that they need to become more robust to meet these demands. You can do this in several ways: by lifting heavier weights, increasing the number of repetitions or sets, enhancing the intensity of your exercises, or even reducing the rest time between sets.

For example, if you start by lifting a 20-pound weight in one workout, you might add an extra five pounds the next time you perform that exercise, or you could keep the same weight but do one more repetition than before. Each slight increase adds a new challenge, encouraging your muscles to build up and adapt.

It's essential to apply progressive overload properly to avoid injury. Increases should be incremental and manageable. If you add too much too quickly, your body won't have time to adapt, leading to strain and injury. The goal is to find the sweet spot where you're pushing yourself just enough to progress without overdoing it.

In practice, keeping a workout journal can be incredibly helpful. It allows you to track how much you're lifting, how many repetitions you do, and how you feel during exercises. This information can guide when to up the ante or even scale back.

Progressive overload isn't just about getting stronger or building muscle; it's about continually challenging yourself to improve your fitness. It keeps your workouts fresh and exciting, pushing you towards your best. Understanding and implementing this principle sets the stage for continued progress and long-term success in your fitness journey.

The role of rest and recovery in strength gains

Rest and recovery are critical components of any strength training program and crucial in gaining strength. While it might seem like constant training is the fastest route to improved stability and muscle growth, the truth is that the time spent out of the gym is just as important as the time spent in it.

When you lift weights or engage in strength training, you create tiny tears in your muscle fibers. This might sound concerning, but it's a natural and essential part of building stronger muscles. The real growth happens not when you're working out but when you're resting. During recovery periods, your body repairs these micro-tears, making the muscles more substantial than they were before. This process requires both time and adequate nutrition—especially proteins, which are the building blocks of muscle.

Skipping rest days can have the opposite effect, such as muscle fatigue, decreased performance, and even injuries. Overtraining can also compromise your immune system, making you more susceptible to illnesses, which could further delay your training progress.

Furthermore, recovery isn't just about taking days off. It includes several practices that can help enhance muscle repair and growth:

Sleep: Quality sleep is perhaps the most effective form of recovery. During sleep, your body produces Growth Hormone (GH), which is essential for muscle growth and repair. Most adults need between 7 and 9 hours of sleep per night to function best, and this is no different for athletes.

Active recovery: This involves performing low-intensity exercise during the recovery days. Activities like walking, yoga, or light cycling help stimulate blood flow to the muscles without straining them, which can help speed up the healing process.

Nutrition: Eating the right balance of nutrients, especially proteins and carbohydrates, helps refuel your body and supplies the necessary materials for muscle repair. Additionally, staying hydrated is crucial, as water plays many roles in the body, including transporting nutrients to the cells and removing waste products from them.

Stretching and mobility work: Gentle stretching or mobility exercises can help maintain a full range of motion and reduce stiffness during recovery. This can also aid in aligning the muscle fibers during the repair process, contributing to better muscle function and growth.

By prioritizing rest and recovery in your training schedule, you ensure your body has the time and resources to repair and strengthen your muscles. This approach enhances your performance over time and minimizes the risk of injury, making your training program sustainable in the long run. Remember, more isn't always better; sometimes, the best thing you can do for your strength gains is to take a step back and allow your body to recuperate.

How to balance training volume with intensity

Balancing training volume and intensity is crucial for optimizing your workouts and achieving the best results without overtraining or burning out. Understanding how to manage these aspects can help you maximize your gym time.

Training volume refers to your total work, often calculated as the number of sets and reps multiplied by the weight used during your session. Intensity, however, relates to how hard those exercises are, typically measured by the percentage of your one-repetition maximum (1RM) or the perceived level of effort during the exercise.

To find the right balance, set a clear goal for each workout. Are you aiming to build strength, increase muscle size, or enhance endurance? Your goal will dictate the approach you take. For instance, strength training typically requires higher intensity with heavier weights and lower volume, meaning fewer reps and sets with more extended rest periods. This allows you to lift more weight since you work closer to your maximum capacity for shorter bursts.

If your goal is muscle hypertrophy or growth, you'd likely shift towards a moderately high volume with moderate intensity. This could be like performing more sets with more repetitions at a moderately challenging weight. The key here is to exhaust the muscles through repeated effort, stimulating growth.

Endurance training takes another step back in intensity. Here, the focus is on a high volume with low intensity. You might use lighter weights but perform more repetitions to increase the time your muscles are under tension, which improves muscular endurance.

It's also important to consider your weekly training load. Distribute the volume and intensity across your workouts so you don't do the most physically taxing sessions back-to-back. Spacing out intense workouts allows for adequate recovery when muscle repair and growth occur.

Listening to your body is vital. If you find yourself constantly fatigued, experiencing a decline in performance, or feeling aches that don't go away, these could be signs of excessive volume or intensity. In such cases, reducing the load or taking extra rest days may be necessary.

Remember that balance is dynamic. What works well one month might need adjustment the next as you get stronger or as your goals evolve. Regularly reassess your training volume and intensity to ensure they align with your current fitness level and goals, adjusting as necessary to keep progressing without overdoing it. This thoughtful approach to balancing volume and intensity helps prevent injuries and ensures sustained progress in your fitness journey.

The importance of consistency over perfection

Consistency is often hailed as one of the most critical factors in the success of any strength training program. While striving for perfection in each workout session can be motivating, regular, consistent effort leads to lasting results and improvement in fitness and strength.

Focusing on consistency rather than perfection means making your workouts a routine. It's about showing up daily, week after week, and not getting hung up on whether every session is flawless or maximal. This approach helps to build a solid foundation of strength, endurance, and muscle memory, which are essential for long-term progress.

Consistency is so powerful because it helps our bodies adapt to stress. Regular exercise consistently demands your muscles, bones, and cardiovascular system, prompting them to strengthen and improve over time. On the other hand, inconsistent workouts don't provide this regular stimulus, making it harder for the body to adapt and improve.

Moreover, consistency in your workouts helps to develop habits. When exercise becomes a habit, it's less likely to be skipped, even when motivation is low. This habitual aspect of regular training can be more beneficial than occasional perfect workouts because it ensures that you are continuously moving towards your fitness goals, regardless of the daily fluctuations in performance or energy levels.

Additionally, focusing on consistency helps alleviate the pressure to perform perfectly in every workout, which can be daunting and unrealistic. This mindset shift can reduce the risk of burnout and injury, which are more common when pushing oneself too hard to pursue an ideal session. It also encourages a more positive and sustainable relationship with exercise, which is crucial for long-term engagement and success.

It's also important to recognize that progress is often nonlinear. Some days, you might feel strong and capable, while others, you might not perform well. A consistent approach allows you to accept these fluctuations as part of the process. Over time, the ups and downs smooth out, and what remains is overall improvement.

Consistency means setting a realistic workout schedule that fits your lifestyle and sticking to it. It involves gradually increasing the intensity and volume of your workouts to continue challenging your body while allowing adequate rest and recovery time.

While striving for perfection can be a compelling motivator, the commitment to consistent effort truly drives substantial and sustainable improvements in strength training. By focusing on making regular exercise a staple of your routine, you lay down the foundations for success and open the door to continuous growth and enhancement of your physical health.

CHAPTER 6

Mastering the form and technique of each exercise is fundamental to any strength training program. Proper technique ensures that you are targeting the right muscles effectively while minimizing the risk of injury. This chapter focuses on the importance of form and technique, providing you with the tools and knowledge needed to execute exercises correctly. Whether you're a beginner learning the basics or an experienced lifter refining your skills, understanding and applying the principles of good form will enhance your training efficiency and safety, helping you achieve your fitness goals more effectively.

Importance of proper form in strength training

Proper form in strength training cannot be overstated, as it is central to achieving effective and safe workouts. Maintaining correct form during exercises ensures that you target the intended muscle groups without placing undue stress on other body parts. This precision not only maximizes the efficacy of your workout but also significantly reduces the risk of injury.

When you lift weights with proper form, you engage the correct muscles in a controlled and deliberate manner. This focus allows for more efficient muscle activation and development, crucial for building strength and muscle mass. For example, performing a squat with proper alignment involves multiple muscle groups, including the glutes, quadriceps, and core. Incorrect form, however, might shift undue stress to the lower back or knees, reducing the effectiveness of the exercise on the target muscles and increasing the likelihood of strain or injury.

Proper form also contributes to better overall body mechanics. This is important not just within the gym setting but also for everyday activities. Good form strengthens the body's natural movement patterns, enhancing balance, coordination, and stability. These benefits translate into improved performance in sports and daily tasks, such as lifting heavy objects or walking stairs.

Moreover, training with the correct form helps ensure that each workout contributes positively to your fitness goals. It allows progressive overload to be applied safely and effectively, which is necessary for continual improvement. As you increase the weight or resistance, maintaining good form becomes even more crucial to handle these greater demands safely.

Proper form also helps prevent the plateau effect, where progress in strength and muscle gain stalls. Often, plateaus occur not from a lack of effort but repeated incorrect movements that fail to adequately challenge the intended muscle groups. By ensuring that each exercise is performed correctly, you can continue to push your limits and see consistent gains.

For those new to strength training, learning and adhering to proper form should be a priority before increasing the weight or complexity of exercises. It's often beneficial to work with a trained professional, at least initially, to learn how to perform movements correctly. Even for experienced lifters, it's valuable to periodically revisit the fundamentals of form to prevent bad habits from creeping in.

Proper form is a cornerstone of effective strength training. It ensures that workouts are efficient, safe, and beneficial in various aspects of physical fitness and daily life. Focusing on technique helps safeguard against injuries, enhances performance, and contributes to achieving long-term fitness objectives efficiently.

Detailed guidance on squats

Squats are a cornerstone exercise in strength training, known for their effectiveness in working the glutes, quadriceps, hamstrings, and core. To get the most out of squats and avoid injury, it's essential to master the correct form.

Start by standing with your feet slightly wider than hip-width apart, toes pointing slightly outward. Extend your arms straight in front of you to help maintain balance. This stance will provide a stable base throughout the exercise.

Begin the squat by deep breathing and tightening your core, which will help stabilize your spine and pelvis. Initiate the movement by shifting your hips as if sitting down in a chair, bending your knees while keeping the weight in your heels. It's crucial to ensure your knees do not extend beyond your toes to keep the strain off your knee joints.

Lower yourself until your thighs are parallel to the floor or as low as your mobility allows without compromising your form. If you're new to squats, you might start by squatting to a shallower depth as you build flexibility and strength.

Throughout the squat, maintain a straight and neutral back, keep your chest lifted, and your gaze forward to help with balance. Ensure your knees stay aligned with your toes and do not cave inward to protect your joints.

To rise back to the starting position, push through your heels, straightening your hips and knees simultaneously. Exhale as you ascend and engage your glutes and thighs to power the movement, keeping your core tight.

Repeat the movement for the desired number of repetitions, maintaining form throughout. As you gain confidence and strength, you can increase the depth of your squat, add repetitions, or introduce weights.

A few common mistakes to avoid include allowing the knees to collapse inward, lifting the heels off the ground, or rounding the back, all of which can lead to injuries.

Always warm up adequately before performing squats to increase joint mobility and decrease the risk of injury. If you have existing knee or back issues or are new to this exercise, consider working with a fitness professional to modify the squat to meet your needs. Once comfortable with your squat form, you may consider adding weights like a barbell or dumbbell to increase the intensity of the exercise.

Detailed guidance on deadlifts

The deadlift is a comprehensive strength training exercise that engages multiple muscle groups, including the glutes, hamstrings, lower back, and core. It's crucial for building strength but requires attention to form to avoid injuries and maximize effectiveness.

To start a deadlift, position yourself with your feet about hip-width apart and toes pointing slightly outward. The barbell should be placed over the middle of your feet, close enough that your shins are nearly touching it. This helps keep the weight centered and balanced.

When you grip the bar, you can choose between a double overhand grip (both palms facing you) or a mixed grip (one palm facing you and one away), depending on what feels more comfortable and the weight you are lifting. Bend at the hips and knees to reach the bar, keeping your back straight and shoulders slightly in front of the bar with your chest up. This posture ensures your spine remains neutral and reduces the risk of injury.

As you begin the lift, focus on engaging your core and maintaining a straight back. Drive the lift through your heels, using the strength of your legs while keeping the bar close to your body. The power should mainly come from your hips and legs rather than your lower back. As the bar passes your knees, push your hips forward and straighten your body to reach a full standing position. Ensure the bar travels vertically and your hips and shoulders rise simultaneously.

To lower the bar back to the ground, reverse the motion. Bend at the hips and guide the bar down the same path it came up, keeping it close to your body. Once the bar is past your knees, you can bend your legs more significantly to place it gently on the ground.

Maintaining correct form throughout the deadlift is crucial. Avoid rounding your back, as this puts excessive stress on the spine. Also, ensure that you lift in a smooth, controlled manner. Jerking the bar can cause a loss of form and control, raising the risk of injury. Keeping the bar close to your body is also essential to minimize leverage on your lower back, which can cause strain.

Deadlifts are beneficial but demanding, and starting with lighter weights to master your technique is advisable. As you gain more confidence and strength, you can gradually increase the weight, always keeping a keen eye on maintaining good form. Using a mirror to check your technique or getting feedback from a coach or trainer can also be very beneficial. As you progress, increasing your weight while prioritizing proper techniques will help you make the most of your workouts safely and effectively.

Detailed guidance on bench presses

The bench press is a classic strength training exercise that targets the chest, shoulders, and triceps. Performing the bench press correctly is crucial for maximizing muscle development and minimizing the risk of injury.

To start, lie on a flat bench with your eyes directly under the barbell. Plant your feet firmly on the floor, with your legs bent. This stable base will help you maintain control throughout the exercise. Grip the bar slightly wider than shoulder-width apart; the exact width can vary slightly depending on your body proportions and what feels most comfortable while allowing effective muscle targeting.

Lift the bar off the rack with the help of a spotter if available, and hold it straight over your chest with your arms fully extended. This is your starting position. Take a deep breath and begin to lower the bar slowly and control. As the bar descends, aim to bring it down evenly until it lightly touches the middle of your chest. During this motion, keep your elbows at about a 45-degree angle to your body to reduce stress on the shoulder joints.

Once the bar touches your chest, push it back to the starting position by extending your arms and exhaling. Drive through your feet and use the strength of your chest and arms to lift the bar. It's essential to move the bar in a controlled manner throughout the lift—avoid jerky movements or bouncing the bar off your chest, as these can lead to injuries.

Here are some key points to keep in mind to ensure you perform the bench press safely and effectively:

- **Maintain a controlled pace**: Lowering the bar slowly helps maintain tension in the chest muscles and increases the exercise's effectiveness.

- **Keep your feet grounded**: Your feet should remain flat on the floor throughout the exercise to help stabilize your body. If your feet are moving or lifting off the ground, it might be a sign that the weight is too heavy.
- **Engage your core**: Activating your core muscles throughout the exercise helps stabilize your entire body and prevents excessive back arching.
- **Avoid lifting your hips off the bench**: Your hips should remain in contact with the bench during the entire exercise. Lifting your hips can put unnecessary strain on your lower back.
- **Use a spotter when lifting heavy** weights: A spotter can assist you if you cannot lift weights, helping prevent injury.

As with any exercise, it's crucial to start with a weight that allows you to maintain good form and gradually increase the load as your strength improves. Regularly practicing the bench press with proper technique will enhance strength and muscle size in the upper body.

Common mistakes and how to correct them

In strength training, making common mistakes can significantly hinder your progress and increase the risk of injury. Recognizing and correcting these errors is crucial for maximizing the effectiveness of your workouts and ensuring your safety. Here's a look at some typical mistakes and how to fix them:

Many individuals skip the warm-up, rushing straight into intense exercise. This oversight can lead to poor performance and increased injury risk as muscles are not adequately prepared. To correct this, always start your workout with at least 5-10 minutes of light cardiovascular activity followed by dynamic stretches. This routine increases blood flow, warms your muscles, and prepares your joints for the workout.

Eagerness to see quick results can lead some to lift heavier weights than they can handle with good form. This often leads to improper technique and can cause injuries. Focus on mastering the form with lighter weights first. Gradually increase the weight only when you can perform the exercise with perfect technique for the desired number of repetitions.

If not checked, using a partial range of motion can become a habit. This practice limits the effectiveness of the exercise by not engaging the muscle throughout its entire length. Ensure you are moving through the full range of motion unless there is a specific reason not to, such as a physical limitation or injury. If unsure, consult a fitness professional to learn the correct range.

Improper breathing during lifting, such as holding your breath or breathing out at the wrong time, can affect performance and even lead to dizziness or other issues. Breathe out during the exertion part of the exercise, which is typically when you lift or push the weight, and breathe in during the easier phase. For example, exhale when pressing a barbell during a bench press and inhale as you lower it.

Working out too frequently without adequate rest can lead to overtraining syndrome, where performance plateaus or declines, and the risk of injury increases. Incorporate rest days in your training regimen to allow recovery and muscle growth. Ensure you are getting enough sleep and managing stress effectively.

Poor posture and lack of core engagement can compromise the effectiveness of your workouts and lead to back pain or other injuries. Actively think about engaging your core during all exercises and maintain good posture. This means keeping your back straight, shoulders back, and chest out. For seated or standing exercises, ensure your spine is neutral.

By being aware of these common mistakes and taking steps to correct them, you can enhance the safety and effectiveness of your strength training program. Remember, consistency in practicing proper technique is just as important as the exercise itself. If you are ever uncertain about your form or technique, don't hesitate to ask for advice from a qualified trainer.

CHAPTER 7

Building a Solid Foundation

Starting a strength training routine can be exciting and overwhelming for beginners. This chapter aims to lay a solid foundation for those new to strength training by providing a structured plan that carefully introduces fundamental exercises. We'll help you develop proper technique and build confidence in your abilities. Focusing on essential principles and gradually increasing the complexity of workouts, this beginner's plan is designed to set you up for long-term success and help you achieve your fitness goals safely and effectively.

Introduction to compound movements

Compound movements engage multiple muscle groups and joints simultaneously, making them highly efficient for building strength and improving overall fitness. These exercises are foundational to any effective strength training program, particularly for beginners, as they provide substantial functional benefits that apply to everyday activities.

One key advantage of compound movements is their ability to simulate real-world movements and activities. Exercises like squats, deadlifts, and bench presses require coordinated muscle contractions that mirror your body's challenges outside the gym, such as lifting heavy objects or pushing against resistance. This makes compound movements not only effective for building muscle and strength but also crucial for enhancing your ability to perform daily tasks with greater ease and less risk of injury.

Additionally, because compound movements work multiple muscles at once, they offer a more time-efficient way to exercise. You can achieve comprehensive muscular engagement in fewer movements instead of performing several isolated exercises to target individual muscle groups. This efficiency is particularly beneficial for beginners who must build a general strength base before moving on to more specialized routines.

Incorporating compound movements into your workout also promotes an excellent hormonal response. Exercises like squats and deadlifts involving large muscle groups can increase the production of hormones like testosterone and human growth hormone, which are essential for muscle growth and overall health.

Furthermore, compound exercises are excellent for caloric burn. Because they engage large parts of the body, they require more energy to perform, making them ideal for those looking to enhance their metabolic rate and burn more calories during and after workouts.

Starting with basic compound movements and learning proper form is crucial for beginners. This ensures safety during exercises and builds a solid foundation of strength that can be expanded upon with more complex movements or heavier weights as your fitness improves. By mastering these fundamental exercises, beginners can maximize their workout effectiveness and pave the way for more advanced fitness challenges.

Designing a beginner's strength training program

Designing a beginner's strength training program involves creating a balanced approach that introduces the fundamentals of strength training in a way that builds confidence and physical fitness gradually. Here's how to craft a practical beginner's strength training regimen:

Focus initially on basic compound movements that work for multiple muscle groups simultaneously, such as squats, deadlifts, bench presses, and overhead presses. These exercises efficiently build functional strength and coordination, making them ideal for beginners.

Plan for 2-3 weekly training sessions to allow for adequate rest and recovery, which are crucial in the early stages of strength training. Each session should last about 45 to 60 minutes, keeping the workouts manageable and not overly daunting.

Incorporate various exercises in each session, ensuring all major muscle groups are engaged throughout the week. You might start with one exercise for each major group—upper body push, upper body pull, lower body pull, lower body pull, and a core exercise.

Begin with lighter weights where you can comfortably perform 8-12 repetitions per set. This range helps build muscular endurance and strength without overloading the muscles too soon. Start with 2-3 sets per exercise, gradually increasing as you gain comfort and stability.

Allow 1-2 minutes of rest between sets and exercises. This rest period is crucial for recovery, especially as you're learning new movements and your body adapts to the stress of weightlifting.

Once you can consistently perform each exercise with good technique, gradually increase the weight while staying within the 8-12 rep range. Depending on your fitness goals, progression can also mean increasing the number of sets or reducing the rest time between sets.

Include basic stretching and mobility exercises at the end of each session. This practice helps maintain joint health, improves flexibility, and can reduce the risk of injuries.

Keep a training log to monitor your progress, noting weights used, sets and reps completed, and how the exercises felt. This record-keeping is invaluable for adjusting the program as you progress, helping to ensure continuous improvement and motivation.

By following these steps, a beginner can develop a solid foundation in strength training, setting the stage for more specialized training as fitness levels improve. This structured yet adaptable approach helps manage the physical demands of training while encouraging consistent progress and minimizing the risk of injury.

Week-by-week progression for 8 weeks

Creating a week-by-week progression plan for an 8-week beginner strength training program helps ensure gradual improvement in fitness and strength, allowing the body to adapt safely to new demands. Here's a simple guideline on how to structure this progression:

Week 1 and 2: Familiarization and Technique Focus

- **Objective:** Learn proper form and technique for key compound exercises like squats, deadlifts, bench presses, and rows.
- **Action:** Start with light weights or body weight to ensure correct form. Perform two sets of 8-10 repetitions for each exercise.
- **Frequency:** Train thrice weekly, with at least one day of rest between sessions.

Week 3 and 4: Gradual Increase in Intensity

- **Objective:** Begin to build strength by increasing weights slightly.
- **Action:** Increase the weight so you can complete 2-3 sets of 8-10 repetitions with moderate effort. Focus on maintaining proper form even with the added weight.
- **Frequency:** Continue with three sessions per week.

Week 5 and 6: Introduction of Additional Sets

- **Objective:** Enhance muscular endurance and strength by adding more volume to the workouts.
- **Action:** Add a set to each exercise, aiming for three sets of 8-10 repetitions. If the form remains consistent, slightly increase the weight.
- **Frequency:** Maintain the three days per week schedule.

Week 7 and 8: Consolidation and Assessment

- **Objective:** Solidify the gains in strength and start assessing improvements.

- **Action:** Continue with three sets and try to increase the weights slightly from the previous weeks. Each session should feel challenging but doable.
- **Frequency:** Stick to the three sessions per week.

It's crucial to listen to your body throughout the eight weeks and adjust accordingly. If a particular weight starts feeling easier, it's a sign that you can increase the weight slightly for the next session. However, if you experience any pain or discomfort, reduce the weights or the number of repetitions to prevent injury.

Flexibility and mobility work should be incorporated at the end of each session to aid recovery and improve performance. This can include static stretching or basic yoga poses, which help.

The eight weeks, evaluate your strength, endurance, and overall fitness progress. Note improvements in how much you can lift, how many repetitions you can perform, and how you feel overall. This assessment will help guide future training decisions and adjustments.

This structured approach ensures you gradually increase the challenge, essential for building strength safely and effectively as a beginner in strength training.

Evaluating progress and making necessary adjustments

Keeping track of your progress and adjusting your strength training program is crucial, especially when starting. This helps ensure you're on track with your fitness goals and allows you to make changes based on your performance.

One effective way to monitor how well you're doing is by keeping a workout diary. In this diary, you can note your exercises, the weights you lift, and how many sets and repetitions you complete. Over time, you should see improvements, like lifting heavier weights or doing more repetitions.

Measuring parts of your body, such as your arms, waist, and hips, can also help if your goal is to change your body size or shape. Using tools to measure your body fat can give you a clearer picture of how your body is transforming.

Taking pictures of yourself regularly can be incredibly motivating. Daily changes might be hard to notice, but photos taken over time can clearly show how much your body has changed.

Performing fitness tests periodically is another excellent way to check your progress. For example, you could see how many push-ups you can do in a minute and compare this number over different periods.

It's also important to pay attention to how you feel overall. If you're getting stronger and feeling more energetic, your program is working well. However, if you constantly feel tired, it might be a sign that you need to adjust your workouts.

If your workouts are becoming too easy or challenging, it might be time to adjust the intensity. If you're not feeling challenged enough, try increasing the weights or adding more repetitions. If the workouts are too hard, reducing the weights or the number of repetitions is perfectly okay.

If you discover that some exercises are more enjoyable or effective, include more of those in your routine. On the other hand, if something doesn't feel right, don't hesitate to replace it with a different exercise.

If certain body parts are not strengthening as expected, you should focus on exercises targeting those areas.

Factors outside the gym, such as your diet, sleep patterns, and stress levels, can also affect your training results. If something in your lifestyle makes your training goals harder to achieve, it's worth taking the time to make some changes.

Regularly checking your progress and making necessary adjustments to your training plan will keep your workouts effective, engaging, and aligned with your fitness goals. This approach ensures that your training remains enjoyable and that you continue to see improvements.

CHAPTER 8

Nutritional Strategies for Muscle Growth and Fat Loss

Proper nutrition plays a pivotal role in achieving any fitness goal, but it is particularly crucial when the objectives include building muscle and losing fat. This chapter delves into the nutritional strategies that support these goals, providing a clear guide on fueling your body effectively to maximize your strength training results. We'll explore the key nutrients needed for muscle repair and growth, discuss the importance of meal timing, and offer practical tips on creating a balanced diet that helps reduce body fat while preserving lean muscle mass. Understanding and applying these nutritional principles can enhance overall fitness and sculpt a more substantial, leaner physique.

Fundamental nutrition for strength training

Understanding fundamental nutrition for strength training is crucial for enhancing muscle growth and overall physical performance. Proper nutrition provides the building blocks your body needs to recover from intense workouts and build stronger muscles.

Protein is a key nutrient in any strength trainer's diet because it is essential for the repair and growth of muscle tissues. After a workout, muscles are essentially broken down, and protein helps repair these fibers, allowing them to grow bigger and stronger. For most people engaged in regular strength training, consuming about 1.2 to 2.0 grams of protein per kilogram of body weight per day is recommended. Good protein sources include lean meats, fish, eggs, dairy products, legumes, and, for those who do not consume animal products, a variety of plant-based proteins such as quinoa and soy.

Carbohydrates are also crucial as they are your body's primary energy source. They fuel your workouts and help with recovery. Including adequate carbohydrates in your diet ensures that your body can perform at its best during training and aids in the recovery process by replenishing glycogen stores in your muscles. Whole grains, fruits, vegetables, and legumes are excellent sources of complex carbohydrates.

Fats should not be neglected either, as they play a vital role in hormone production, including hormones like testosterone and human growth hormone, which are crucial for muscle growth. Healthy fats also help your body absorb essential vitamins and provide a good energy source for less intense, longer-duration exercises. Include sources of healthy fats such as avocados, nuts, seeds, and olive oil in your diet.

Hydration is another critical aspect of nutrition for strength training. Water helps transport nutrients to your cells, keeps joints lubricated, and regulates body temperature during workouts. Drinking sufficient water throughout the day is vital, especially before, during, and after exercise, to prevent dehydration.

In addition to what to eat, when you eat can also impact your training results. Consuming a mix of proteins and carbohydrates shortly after a workout, often referred to as the anabolic window, can maximize muscle recovery and growth by taking advantage of your body's heightened ability to absorb and utilize these nutrients post-exercise.

While focusing on macronutrients (proteins, carbohydrates, fats) and hydration, don't overlook micronutrients. Vitamins and minerals like iron, calcium, and vitamins D and B12 are crucial for practical strength training in energy production, oxygen transportation, and bone health.

Balancing these nutritional elements, you can create a diet that supports your strength training efforts and contributes to your overall health and well-being. This holistic approach to nutrition ensures that you're not just building muscle but also enhancing your body's recovery and resilience, setting the stage for long-term fitness and health.

Hydration and its importance

Hydration is critical to your strength training regimen's overall effectiveness and health. Water is essential for numerous bodily functions, including muscle function, joint lubrication, nutrient transport, and temperature regulation. When adequately hydrated, your body performs these functions efficiently, particularly during exercise.

During strength training, your muscles generate heat, which increases your body temperature. Water helps regulate this heat through sweating and respiration, preventing overheating and maintaining optimal body temperature for performance. If you're not adequately hydrated, your body's ability to manage heat is compromised, leading to decreased performance, early fatigue, and even heat-related illnesses such as heatstroke.

Moreover, hydration is crucial for maintaining blood volume and pressure, ensuring enough oxygen and nutrients are delivered to your muscles during a workout. When dehydrated, your blood volume decreases, reducing your body's ability to transport oxygen and nutrients efficiently. This can result in muscle fatigue and reduced strength, limiting the effectiveness of your training session.

Water also plays a key role in joint health. It helps keep the cartilage soft and hydrated, which reduces friction and wear during exercise, potentially lowering the risk of joint injuries. Proper hydration can, therefore, help enhance mobility and reduce pain during exercises that put a lot of stress on joints, like squats and deadlifts.

Staying hydrated before, during, and after workouts ensures optimal performance and recovery. Before exercising, try to drink at least 15 to 20 ounces of water about one to two hours beforehand to start adequately hydrating. During exercise, drink about 7 to 10 ounces every 10 to 20 minutes, especially during intense or prolonged sessions. After finishing your workout, replenish any fluid lost by drinking water or a sports drink that can also help replace electrolytes if the exercise duration exceeds an hour or occurs in hot and humid conditions.

Being mindful of the color of your urine is a practical way to monitor your hydration status. A pale yellow indicates good hydration, whereas a dark yellow or amber might suggest dehydration.

Staying adequately hydrated is a simple yet crucial aspect of your training regimen that can significantly affect your strength training outcomes. It enhances your performance, aids in recovery and muscle function, and helps prevent injuries, making it essential for anyone looking to optimize their fitness routine.

Using supplements wisely

Using supplements wisely is essential for anyone involved in strength training, especially those looking to enhance performance, improve recovery, and support overall health. While supplements can be beneficial, it's crucial to approach them with a thoughtful and informed strategy.

Firstly, it's essential to recognize that supplements should supplement your diet, not replace whole food sources. A well-balanced diet rich in proteins, carbohydrates, fats, vitamins, and minerals is foundational. Supplements should only be used to fill nutritional gaps or enhance certain aspects of your training and recovery.

One of the most commonly used supplements in strength training is protein powder. Protein is essential for muscle repair and growth, and while it should ideally come from food sources like meats, beans, and dairy, protein powders can be a convenient way to ensure you meet your daily protein needs, especially post-workout when your body needs protein the most for muscle recovery.

Creatine is another popular supplement known for its benefits in increasing power output and muscle endurance, which can be particularly useful during high-intensity training sessions. Creatine works by increasing the availability of ATP, a key energy source for muscle contractions, and can also help with quicker recovery between sets.

Branched-chain amino acids (BCAAs) often reduce muscle breakdown during exercise, speed recovery, and improve exercise performance. BCAAs refer to three essential amino acids - leucine, isoleucine, and valine - that the body must obtain from food or supplements.

Beta-alanine can be beneficial for those focusing on endurance along with strength training. It helps increase muscle carnosine levels, which supports muscle endurance by reducing fatigue and may improve overall exercise performance.

While these supplements can be helpful, it's essential to use them judiciously:

- **Research**: Understand what each supplement does and the evidence supporting its use. Not all supplements are created equal; some can have side effects or interact with other medications.
- **Quality**: Choose high-quality, well-tested products from reputable manufacturers to avoid contaminants and ensure you get what the label claims.
- **Dosage**: Follow dosage recommendations carefully. More is not always better, and excessive intake of some supplements can be harmful.
- **Consult with Professionals**: Before starting any supplement regimen, especially if you have underlying health conditions or are taking medications, consult a healthcare provider or a nutritionist.

While supplements can help enhance some aspects of your training, they are not magic pills. Real and sustainable gains in strength, muscle mass, and overall fitness come from consistent training, proper nutrition, adequate rest, and hydration. Supplements should be seen as an adjunct to these foundational elements, not as a substitute for them.

Meal planning tips for muscle growth and fat loss

Meal planning is essential for optimizing their strength training results, mainly when the goals include muscle growth and fat loss. Effective meal planning ensures you're consuming the right balance of nutrients at appropriate times to fuel your workouts and aid recovery while managing your caloric intake to support your body composition goals. Here are some practical tips for meal planning that can help you build muscle and lose fat:

Balance your macronutrients in each meal. Proteins are crucial for muscle repair and growth, so include good protein sources like chicken, fish, lean beef, eggs, and plant-based options such as beans and lentils. Carbohydrates provide the energy needed for your workouts and recovery, so choose complex carbs like whole grains, sweet potatoes, and various vegetables, especially around your training sessions. Don't forget about healthy fats, vital for hormone production and overall health, sourced from avocados, nuts, seeds, and olive oil.

Timing your nutrient intake can also enhance your training results. On days when you are training hard, increase your carbohydrate intake to fuel and recover from the workouts. You might reduce your carbohydrate intake slightly on rest days or lighter activity days, as your energy demand is lower.

Managing portions and calories is key whether your goal is muscle growth or fat loss. For muscle growth, you should consume more calories than you burn to maintain a surplus. Aim for a caloric deficit for fat loss by consuming fewer calories than you burn. Tracking your intake using a food diary or calorie-tracking app can help you adjust your diet based on your progress and specific goals.

Prepping your meals in advance can help you stay on track with your nutritional goals. It makes healthy choices readily available and helps you avoid the temptation of less healthy foods. Cook meals in bulk and store them in portion-controlled containers to simplify your meal routine.

Focus on whole, unprocessed foods to maximize nutrient intake and improve satiety. These foods are generally more filling, which can help manage hunger and reduce overall calorie intake, supporting fat loss.

Hydration should not be overlooked. Drinking enough water is crucial for overall health, metabolism optimization, and muscle recovery. Ensure you drink plenty of water throughout the day, not just during and after workouts.

Including a snack or meal that combines protein and carbohydrates shortly after your workout can significantly enhance muscle recovery and energy replenishment, preparing you for the next workout.

Listen to your body's responses to different foods and their timing. Adjust your meal planning based on how you feel during workouts, your recovery quality, and overall progress toward your goals.

Tailoring your meal planning to support your workout efforts and body goals can greatly enhance muscle growth and fat loss. This ensures that your hard work in the gym is effectively supported by optimal nutrition.

CHAPTER 9

Advanced Techniques and Plateau Breaking

As you progress in your strength training journey, the gains you once experienced have begun to slow down or even stall. This is a common challenge known as hitting a plateau. This chapter will explore various advanced training techniques and strategies to help you break through these plateaus and continue progressing. From altering your exercise routine to incorporating new and more challenging techniques, this chapter will provide the tools and knowledge needed to keep advancing your fitness goals, ensuring that your workouts remain effective and engaging.

When and how to incorporate advanced lifting techniques

As you gain experience in strength training and your foundational strength improves, incorporating advanced lifting techniques can significantly enhance muscle growth, increase strength, and break through plateaus. However, knowing when and how to integrate these techniques safely and effectively into your routine is essential.

Advanced lifting techniques, such as drop sets, supersets, and pyramids, are typically used by those who have already developed good muscle strength and coordination and a solid understanding of exercise form. It's generally advisable to start using these techniques after you have at least several months of consistent training under your belt. This base fitness level ensures that your body is adequately prepared to handle the increased stress and intensity these methods demand.

Drop sets involve continuing an exercise with a lower weight once muscle fatigue sets in at a higher weight. For example, if you're doing bicep curls with 30 pounds and can no longer complete reps with good form, you might drop to 20 pounds and continue until you hit fatigue again. This method helps push the muscles beyond the typical fatigue point experienced in a standard set, encouraging deeper muscle fiber activation and growth.

Supersets combine two exercises performed back to back with no rest in between. They can be for the same muscle group, opposing muscle groups, or completely unrelated muscle groups. By keeping your muscles under continuous stress for more extended periods, supersets save time and increase the intensity of your workout.

Pyramid sets involve gradually increasing or decreasing the weight with each set of exercises. Starting with a lighter weight and higher reps and then increasing the weight while reducing the reps can help build muscular endurance and strength. Alternatively, reverse pyramid training starts with heavy weights for fewer reps and reduces the weight to allow more reps with successive sets.

When incorporating these advanced techniques, it's crucial to maintain focus on proper form to avoid injury. Since these methods can be very demanding, they should not be used for every workout. Instead, integrate them periodically to 'shock' the muscles or when you feel you are not making the desired progress.

Because advanced techniques can significantly increase muscle strain and fatigue, they should be paired with adequate recovery strategies, including increased protein intake, plenty of hydration, and sufficient rest days to allow for muscle repair and growth.

Using these advanced techniques wisely can significantly enhance your strength training routine, helping you overcome plateaus and achieve continued growth and improve your physical fitness.

Using drop sets for intensity

Drop sets are an effective technique for increasing the intensity of your workouts, which can lead to enhanced muscle growth and endurance. This method involves performing an exercise until failure—or close to it—then immediately reducing the weight and continuing to do more repetitions until you can no longer maintain proper form.

The process of using drop sets starts with selecting an initial weight that is heavy enough to perform your exercise with the correct form but also challenging enough that you can only complete a limited number of repetitions. For example, if you're working on bicep curls, you might start with a weight that allows you to do 8-10 reps before your muscles reach fatigue.

Once you reach muscle failure, quickly reduce the weight by approximately 20-30% and continue doing more repetitions without resting. This might mean dropping from 30 pounds to 20-25 pounds on the dumbbells. The key is to perform the additional sets rapidly to keep the muscles under continuous stress.

You can repeat this process of reducing the weight and continuing to work until failure for several "drops. " Usually, 2-3 drops are sufficient for one exercise. Each drop aims to push the muscles slightly beyond their usual limit, which can help break down muscle fibers more effectively, a process essential for muscle growth.

Drop sets are particularly useful when you feel you've hit a plateau with standard sets. They help to significantly increase the volume and intensity of your workout. This sudden increase in demand can stimulate muscle growth and strength gains that might not be achievable through traditional methods alone.

However, because drop sets can tax the muscles, they should be used sparingly. Overusing this technique can lead to overtraining and excessive muscle fatigue, which might hinder your overall progress rather than help it. It's recommended to incorporate drop sets into your routine for one or two exercises per workout, preferably at the end of your session to ensure you don't compromise your energy and form for subsequent exercises.

Proper recovery is crucial when incorporating drop sets into your training. Ensure you are getting enough protein to aid muscle repair, and allow adequate rest for the muscle groups that were intensely worked, as they will need more recovery time than after a standard workout.

Integrating drop sets appropriately and considering overall workout intensity and recovery can significantly enhance your strength training results, pushing through plateaus and increasing muscle endurance and growth.

Employing supersets for endurance

Supersets are an advanced training technique where you perform two exercises back-to-back without resting in between. This method is especially effective for building endurance and increasing the intensity of your workouts. Using supersets, you can maximize your gym time, enhance cardiovascular and muscular endurance, and promote significant muscle growth.

When targeting endurance, you can structure supersets in several different ways. One approach is to perform two exercises that work the same muscle group consecutively, known as agonist supersets. An example would be bench presses followed immediately by push-ups. This approach leads to deep muscle fatigue and increased endurance because of the extended tension and high workload on the same muscle group.

Another strategy involves exercises that target opposing muscle groups, known as antagonist supersets. For instance, you could pair bicep curls with tricep dips. This pairing allows one muscle group to rest while the other works, enabling quicker recovery times and the ability to perform more exercises within a shorter period, which is great for both strength and endurance gains.

To incorporate supersets effectively for boosting endurance, consider these tips:

Choose exercises that you are comfortable performing even as you become fatigued. Maintaining good form throughout, particularly as your muscles tire, is crucial to preventing injury.

Since the aim is to increase endurance, select moderate weights that allow you to complete more repetitions, usually around 12-15 per set. This rep range helps build endurance and ensures you do significant work through your muscles.

Recovery is key when using supersets because they can be very demanding. Ensure you stay well-hydrated, eat a balanced diet rich in proteins and carbohydrates, and get plenty of rest. These recovery strategies help your muscles repair and rebuild, readying you for your next training session.

Keep your workouts varied. Change the exercises you include in your supersets every few weeks to continue challenging your muscles and improving. This helps prevent your progress from plateauing and keeps your workouts exciting and challenging.

Integrating supersets into your training routine can significantly enhance the efficiency and effectiveness of your workouts. This technique pushes your muscles to endure more extended work periods and recover more quickly, improving your overall muscular endurance and fitness levels while potentially cutting down your total workout time.

Recognizing and overcoming plateaus

When you engage in any consistent workout routine, hitting a plateau—where you see no noticeable improvements in strength, muscle growth, or performance—can be a common and frustrating experience. However, recognizing when you've hit a plateau and knowing how to overcome it is crucial to continue your progress in strength training.

A plateau typically occurs because your body has adapted to the current training regimen. The exercises, weights, repetitions, and sets that once challenged your muscles are no longer effective in stimulating growth because your body has become efficient at handling these demands.

You might notice that your strength levels have stagnated; you're unable to lift heavier weights or perform more repetitions. You may also feel less challenged by your workouts and see no physical changes in muscle size or body composition despite your continued efforts.

To overcome a plateau, consider changing your exercise routine. Altering the types of exercises you do, the order in which you perform them, or the groups of muscles you focus on each day can provide the stimulus your muscles need to adapt and grow.

Increasing the intensity of your workouts helps push past a plateau. This might involve lifting heavier weights, increasing the volume of your workouts (more sets or reps), or incorporating advanced techniques like supersets, drop sets, or pyramid sets.

Experimenting with different repetition and set schemes can also be effective. If you typically do three sets of ten, try four sets of six with a heavier weight or two sets of fifteen for endurance.

Sometimes a plateau is a sign that you're not giving your body enough time to recover. Ensuring you get enough sleep, managing stress, and paying attention to your nutrition—especially your intake of proteins and carbohydrates—can improve recovery and performance.

Periodization involves planning variations in your training program over specific periods. It helps manage fatigue, ensures continuous progression, and avoids overtraining by cycling through loading, intensity, and recovery phases.

If you're struggling to overcome a plateau on your own, consider seeking the guidance of a personal trainer or a coach. They can provide an external perspective on your training regimen and offer adjustments that might not be obvious. They can also help tailor your program more precisely to your fitness goals.

A plateau often requires reinvigorating your body's response to training. By introducing new challenges, you can ensure that your workouts remain effective and engaging, pushing you towards higher levels of fitness and closer to your strength training goals.

CHAPTER 10

Strength Training During Pregnancy and Postpartum

Strength training during pregnancy and the postpartum period can be incredibly beneficial, supporting overall health, enhancing mood, and improving physical endurance, which can be crucial both during and after pregnancy. However, it's essential to approach exercise during these times with care to ensure safety and effectiveness. This chapter guides you on safely incorporating strength training into your routine during pregnancy and how to return to exercise after childbirth gradually. We'll cover modifications for each trimester, highlight essential safety tips, and discuss how to listen to your body's unique needs during this transformative time. By understanding the specific considerations and benefits of strength training during these stages, you can maintain your fitness while supporting your and your baby's health.

First trimester workouts

During the first trimester of pregnancy, it's crucial to approach strength training cautiously as your body undergoes significant changes. Maintaining an exercise routine can offer numerous benefits, such as reduced pregnancy-related discomforts, improved mood, and better sleep. Still, modifying your activities to ensure your safety and that of your baby is essential.

Before continuing or starting a new exercise routine during this time, it's essential to consult with your healthcare provider to ensure that strength training is safe for you, especially if there are any complications or risks associated with your pregnancy.

When working out, focus on maintaining a moderate intensity. You should be able to speak comfortably during your exercises, indicating that you're not overexerting yourself. Concentrate on full-body workouts that include exercises for major muscle groups such as the legs, back, arms, and shoulders. However, be cautious with heavy weights. Opting for lighter weights and higher repetitions can help prevent putting too much strain on your body.

It's also wise to avoid high-risk activities. Avoid exercises that involve lying flat on your back for extended periods, as this can restrict blood flow. Additionally, avoid activities that carry a risk of falling or abdominal trauma, such as heavy lifting or exercises that require great balance.

Listening to your body is crucial during this time. Pregnancy can lead to changes in balance and coordination, so adjust your routine as necessary. If you experience any discomfort, such as dizziness, shortness of breath, or pain, stop exercising immediately and consult your healthcare provider.

Stay well-hydrated during workouts and avoid exercising in hot or humid conditions to prevent overheating, which can be dangerous during pregnancy.

Incorporating exercises to strengthen the pelvic floor is also essential during pregnancy, as these muscles support the uterus, bladder, and bowels. Simple exercises like Kegels can be done daily to maintain pelvic floor health.

Second-trimester modifications

As you enter the second trimester of pregnancy, you might find yourself with more energy than in the first trimester, but it remains essential to continue adapting your strength training to meet your body's evolving needs. During this stage, your baby grows more extensive, and your body undergoes significant changes that can affect your center of gravity and overall mobility.

Your balance may be affected by the shifting of your center of gravity due to a growing belly. Exercise caution with movements that require significant balance or might pose a risk of falling. Opt for exercises that provide stability, and consider using supports like a chair or a wall for exercises that involve standing.

Your core also needs attention during this time. As your belly expands, avoid exercises that involve lying on your back for extended periods, as this can compress major blood vessels and reduce circulation to your heart and your baby. Modify your core workouts to safer positions during pregnancy, such as seated, standing, or lying on your side, focusing on gentle strengthening that supports your back.

When lifting weights, continue with light to moderate weights, focusing more on maintaining muscle tone rather than building it further. Incorporating flexibility exercises, such as prenatal yoga, can help manage back pain and improve circulation, both beneficial during pregnancy.

Be cautious about stretching. Pregnancy increases the levels of relaxin, a hormone that loosens ligaments and joints, increasing the risk of injuries. Avoid overstretching and maintain a comfortable and safe range of motion.

Hydration becomes even more crucial during the second trimester. Drink plenty of water before, during, and after your workouts to stay hydrated. Also, ensure that your workout environment is well-ventilated to avoid overheating, as your body temperature is naturally higher during pregnancy.

Always listen to your body and be responsive to its signals. If you feel uncomfortable or experience pain, dizziness, or shortness of breath during exercise, stop immediately and consult with your healthcare provider.

Regular visits to your healthcare provider are essential to ensure your exercise routine remains appropriate as your pregnancy progresses. These check-ups help monitor your health and your baby's, allowing for adjustments in your workout regimen.

By carefully adjusting your strength training routine during the second trimester, you can continue to enjoy the benefits of exercise while ensuring safety for both you and your growing baby and preparing yourself for the demands of childbirth and recovery.

Third-trimester considerations

During the third trimester of pregnancy, as your body prepares for childbirth, it's essential to continue adapting your exercise routine to accommodate further changes and increased demands. This period often brings more discomfort, more significant shifts in balance and mobility, and increased fatigue, making it crucial to adjust your approach to strength training.

As the baby grows and your belly expands significantly, your center of gravity shifts even more, impacting your balance and mobility. It's vital to prioritize safety to prevent falls. Focus on low-impact exercises that can be performed with stable support. Activities like stationary cycling, water aerobics, or gentle prenatal yoga can be good alternatives, offering both safety and adequate exercise.

Exercise intensity should be reduced during the third trimester. The focus should be on maintaining mobility and muscle tone rather than improving fitness or strength. It's a good time to incorporate more stretching and flexibility exercises, which can help relieve discomforts like back pain and enhance circulation. However, remember to move within a comfortable range of motion, as ligaments and joints are still more susceptible to strain due to hormonal changes.

Avoiding any exercises that require lying flat on your back is essential, as this position can restrict blood flow to both you and your baby. Instead, opt for exercises that can be performed while seated, standing, or using a stability ball to provide support without compromising blood flow.

If fatigue becomes a factor, keep sessions shorter and less frequent. Listen to your body's needs and allow more time for rest and recovery. Staying active is beneficial, but conserving energy as you near childbirth is equally essential.

Hydration continues to be extremely important. Drink fluids before, during, and after exercising to stay hydrated. Also, ensure your exercise environment is calm and well-ventilated to help manage body temperature and comfort.

As always, consult with your healthcare provider throughout the third trimester. They can provide personalized advice and adjustments based on your specific health conditions and how your pregnancy is progressing. This is especially important as you approach your due date, as certain types of exercise may become more restrictive.

Carefully managing your strength training and overall exercise routine during the third trimester can help maintain your health and well-being, alleviate pregnancy symptoms, and prepare your body for the physical demands of childbirth.

Postpartum recovery and strength rebuilding

Postpartum recovery and strength rebuilding are critical phases following a child's birth. After delivery, your body needs time to heal and adjust back to its pre-pregnancy state, which can take weeks or even months. Gradually reintroducing exercise can help strengthen muscles weakened during pregnancy, improve overall physical fitness, and boost mental well-being.

The first step in postpartum recovery is to get clearance from your healthcare provider before starting any exercise program. This is typically around 6 weeks after childbirth, but the timing can vary based on individual health conditions and the nature of the delivery (vaginal or cesarean).

Once you have the green light to begin exercising, start slowly. Your body has undergone significant changes and stress, so it's important to ease back into physical activity. Begin with gentle movements like walking or pelvic floor exercises. Walking is a low-impact activity that can help improve cardiovascular fitness and mood without stressing your recovering body. Pelvic floor exercises (often referred to as Kegels) are crucial for strengthening the muscles that support the uterus, bladder, and bowels, especially after they've been stretched and weakened during pregnancy.

As you regain strength and confidence, gradually incorporate more structured exercise routines. Focus on core strengthening exercises to rebuild abdominal strength, essential for overall stability and can help with back pain issues commonly experienced postpartum. Exercises like modified planks, pelvic tilts, and specific yoga poses can be practical. However, be cautious with traditional crunches or sit-ups immediately postpartum, especially if you have diastasis recti (separation of the abdominal muscles).

Strength training can also be reintroduced, starting with light weights or bodyweight exercises. Target major muscle groups with exercises that do not strain the lower back or pelvic area. Resistance bands can be useful tools, as they provide adjustable resistance and can help maintain proper form.

Listen to your body as you progress. Postpartum recovery varies for everyone, and paying attention to any signs of discomfort or pain is essential. If something feels wrong, stop and consult with your healthcare provider.

Staying hydrated, eating a balanced diet rich in nutrients, and getting enough sleep are equally important as they significantly impact your recovery and energy levels.

Rebuilding strength postpartum is not just about getting back into shape but also about nurturing your body's recovery after childbirth. By taking a gradual and mindful approach, you can enhance your physical recovery, support your mental health, and better enjoy the new demands of motherhood.

CHAPTER 11

Strength Training for Mature Women

As women age, strength training becomes essential for maintaining muscle mass and strength and enhancing overall health and quality of life. For mature women, engaging in a tailored strength training program can help combat the natural decline in bone density, muscle strength, and metabolic rate accompanying aging. This chapter focuses on the specific needs and considerations for strength training in mature women, offering guidance on creating effective workout routines that are safe, sustainable, and supportive of long-term health goals. We'll explore modifications, appropriate exercises, and strategies to maximize the benefits of strength training while minimizing the risk of injury, ensuring that women can remain active, independent, and strong throughout their later years.

Adapting strength training during menopause

Adapting strength training during menopause is crucial as this phase brings significant hormonal changes that can impact muscle mass, bone density, and overall strength. Menopause often leads to a decrease in estrogen levels, which can contribute to the loss of bone density and muscle strength, making women more susceptible to osteoporosis and muscle atrophy. Therefore, adapting your strength training routine to address these changes is vital for maintaining health and functionality.

First, it is essential to focus on resistance training that emphasizes muscle strength and bone health. Weight-bearing exercises, such as squats, lunges, and overhead presses, are particularly beneficial as they help stimulate bone growth and improve muscle mass. Various resistance training exercises using free weights, resistance bands, or body weights can effectively target all major muscle groups, enhancing overall strength and endurance.

Adjusting the intensity and volume of workouts may also be necessary during menopause. Women might find that recovery takes longer or experience more fatigue than before. Listening to your body and adjusting the training load is essential. This might mean reducing the weights used, altering the number of sets and repetitions, or increasing rest periods between exercises to allow for adequate recovery.

Flexibility and balance training become increasingly crucial during menopause as well. Yoga and Pilates can be excellent additions to strength training routines. These practices improve flexibility, core strength, and balance, which can help prevent falls and related injuries, which are a higher risk as bone density declines.

In addition to physical adjustments to the training regimen, paying close attention to nutrition can help manage menopause symptoms and enhance training outcomes. Ensure a diet rich in calcium, vitamin D, and protein supports bone health and muscle repair. Staying hydrated is also crucial, as hydration affects joint lubrication and muscle function.

It is advisable to regularly consult with healthcare providers to tailor exercise and dietary plans based on individual health needs and any menopause-related conditions. This personalized approach helps manage symptoms effectively and maintain a high quality of life during and after menopause.

By adapting strength training to their specific needs during menopause, women can significantly mitigate some of the adverse effects of aging, maintain strength, flexibility, and overall health, and continue to lead active, vibrant lives.

Strategies for bone health and osteoporosis prevention

During menopause and beyond, women face an increased risk of osteoporosis due to the decline in estrogen levels, which significantly impacts bone density. To combat this, it's essential to adopt comprehensive strategies encompassing diet, lifestyle, exercise, and potentially medical interventions to enhance bone health and prevent osteoporosis.

Engaging in regular weight-bearing and resistance exercises is crucial. Activities such as walking, jogging, dancing, lifting weights, or using resistance bands are beneficial as they force your body to work against gravity, stimulating bone cells to grow and strengthen. Aim to include these activities in your routine at least 3 to 4 times a week to help improve bone density and overall strength.

Adequate calcium intake is vital for maintaining strong bones. Include calcium-rich foods in your diet, such as dairy products, leafy green vegetables, and calcium-fortified foods. If you suspect your dietary intake may not meet your daily calcium needs, consider discussing calcium supplements with your healthcare provider.

Vitamin D is also essential for calcium absorption in the body. While sunlight is a natural source of vitamin D, aging can reduce the skin's ability to synthesize it effectively. To supplement sunlight exposure, include vitamin D-rich foods such as fatty fish, liver, and eggs, and consider vitamin D supplements based on your doctor's recommendation.

Lifestyle modifications can significantly impact bone health. Quitting smoking and limiting alcohol consumption can mitigate adverse effects on bone density and support overall well-being.

Regular bone density tests are essential for early detection of osteoporosis. Consult with your healthcare provider about the appropriate time to start and the frequency of these tests.

Incorporating balance and coordination exercises can help prevent falls, which are a significant risk factor for bone fractures. Exercises like tai chi or simple balance-enhancing activities can improve stability and reduce the risk of falls.

Protein plays a key role in bone health and muscle maintenance. To support bone repair and growth, ensure your diet includes sufficient protein from a variety of sources, both animal and plant-based.

Staying hydrated is essential for maintaining the health and function of all cells, including bone cells. Ensure you drink adequate fluids throughout the day to support overall cellular functions.

If you are taking medications that could impact bone density, such as corticosteroids, discuss potential alternatives or strategies with your doctor to mitigate these effects.

Integrating these strategies into your daily life can significantly enhance your bone health and reduce the risk of osteoporosis, thereby maintaining your independence and quality of life as you age.

Modifications for age-related physical changes

As women age, physical changes such as decreased bone density, muscle mass, and joint flexibility can affect their ability to perform strength training exercises as they once did. Recognizing these changes and making appropriate modifications to the exercise routine is essential to maintain safety, effectiveness, and enjoyment in training.

Adjusting the exercise intensity is crucial as muscle strength and endurance may decrease with age. This might involve using lighter weights or reducing the number of sets and repetitions to avoid overstressing the body, ensuring that exercises are still challenging but not overwhelming.

Incorporating low-impact exercises can help reduce joint strain, which may have become more vulnerable with age. Activities like swimming, cycling, or using an elliptical machine can strengthen muscles and bones effectively without causing discomfort that might come from high-impact exercises like running or jumping.

Muscles and joints may require more time to warm up and reach complete flexibility as the body ages. Extending the warm-up period with gentle stretching and light aerobic activity can help prepare the body for exercise, reducing the risk of injuries.

Enhancing flexibility training by incorporating more activities such as yoga or Pilates can counteract the stiffness and stability issues often accompanying aging. These practices improve flexibility, balance, and core strength, crucial for maintaining overall mobility and independence.

It is also essential to focus on exercises that mimic daily activities. Squatting, reaching, or lifting are necessary for functional fitness. These exercises help maintain the ability to perform everyday tasks more efficiently and safely, preserving independence.

As recovery times may increase with age, monitoring and adapting rest periods between exercises and workouts is essential. Allowing more time for the body to recuperate between strenuous activities can prevent fatigue and overuse injuries.

Another key consideration is using proper equipment. Ensuring any equipment suitable for your strength and fitness levels can help maintain proper form and reduce the risk of injuries. Adjustable machines tailored to your size and strength are handy.

Working with a fitness professional with experience training older adults can provide valuable guidance. They can offer personalized adjustments and techniques tailored to individual needs, helping to ensure that strength training remains a beneficial and safe part of one's lifestyle as one age.

Keeping motivated in later years

Staying motivated to continue strength training in later years can be challenging as physical changes and the demands of daily life evolve. However, maintaining an active lifestyle is crucial for enhancing quality of life, promoting health, and sustaining independence as you age. Here are several strategies that can help keep motivation high for continuing strength training and exercise into the later years.

Setting achievable goals tailored to your current fitness level and interests can provide clear direction and a sense of purpose. These goals could range from improving posture and enhancing balance to increasing walking endurance or comfortably lifting a set of weights. Achieving these goals gives a sense of accomplishment and can motivate you to set new challenges.

It's also beneficial to remind yourself of the benefits of staying active, such as improved mobility, reduced risk of chronic diseases, better mental health, and enhanced social interactions. Recognizing how your activities contribute to a healthier lifestyle can be a powerful motivator.

Finding activities you enjoy, whether a dance class, yoga, swimming, or group fitness classes geared towards seniors, can make exercise more enjoyable and something to look forward to. Establishing a consistent routine helps embed physical activity into your daily life, making it a regular part of your schedule. Setting workout times can reduce the need for daily decision-making about when or whether to exercise.

Joining exercise groups or classes can provide social encouragement and accountability, which are great motivators. Working out with peers who share similar challenges and goals can enhance your commitment to a fitness regimen, making it more enjoyable and sustainable.

Vary your workout routine regularly to prevent boredom and tackle plateaus. Trying new exercises or changing your workout environment can reinvigorate your interest and challenge different muscle groups, enhancing physical and mental engagement.

Fitness trackers and apps can provide feedback on your progress and achievements. Many apps also offer virtual classes, motivational rewards, and social features that connect you with other users for support and competition.

Recognize and celebrate your achievements, no matter how small. Setting milestones and rewarding yourself for reaching them can boost your sense of accomplishment and encourage you to continue pushing forward.

Regular consultations with fitness professionals specializing in senior fitness can provide personalized advice and modifications that align with your health needs and fitness level. They can help you safely maximize the benefits of your exercise routine and keep you motivated with professional guidance and support.

Focusing on exercise's positive impacts, integrating enjoyable activities into your routine, and utilizing the support of communities and professionals can help you maintain an active and fulfilling lifestyle that significantly contributes to your overall well-being in later years.

CHAPTER 12

Injury Prevention and Management

Strength training brings many health benefits but also carries the risk of injuries, mainly if exercises are performed incorrectly or without adequate preparation. This chapter will explore essential strategies for preventing injuries during strength training and effectively managing them if they occur. This chapter provides comprehensive guidance from proper warm-up routines and using correct form during exercises to understanding the signs of overtraining and how to respond to injuries. It aims to equip you with the knowledge to train safely and maintain a long-term, injury-free exercise regimen. By prioritizing injury prevention and knowing how to handle injuries when they happen, you can ensure more sustainable and effective strength training outcomes.

Common strength training injuries

Understanding common strength training injuries is crucial for fitness or athletic training. Recognizing these injuries and their root causes can significantly aid prevention and ensure a safer workout environment.

One frequent injury is muscle strains, which occur when muscles are overstretched or torn. This often happens during heavy lifting or when performing exercises without proper warm-up. Muscle strains are prevalent in the back, shoulders, and hamstrings.

Another typical injury involves the joints, especially the knees and shoulders. These injuries can result from improper form, overuse, or from performing complex movements without adequate strength or mobility. Examples include rotator cuff tears in the shoulder and anterior cruciate ligament (ACL) injuries in the knee.

Tendonitis, the inflammation of a tendon, is also a common issue. It often results from repetitive use of a particular muscle group without adequate rest, leading to overuse injuries such as tennis elbow or jumper's knee.

Stress fractures are another concern, particularly in weight-bearing activities. These occur when muscles become fatigued and cannot absorb added shock, eventually transferring the stress overload to the bone and creating a tiny crack. This type of injury is common in athletes who perform a lot of running or jumping but can also affect weightlifters.

Preventative measures are key to avoiding these types of injuries. This includes using proper form and technique during exercises, ensuring adequate warm-up and cool-down routines, gradually increasing the intensity and volume of workouts, and incorporating rest days into your fitness regimen to allow muscles and joints to recover.

Additionally, wearing appropriate footwear and using the correct equipment can prevent injuries by providing the necessary support and stability during various exercises.

Listening to your body is essential. Paying attention to signs of pain and discomfort and responding appropriately by adjusting or halting your exercise regimen can prevent minor issues from becoming serious injuries. Regular consultation with fitness professionals for guidance on form and training programs can further enhance your understanding and execution of safe strength training practices.

Effective warm-ups and cool-downs

Effective warm-ups and cool-downs are crucial components of any strength training regimen. They play a significant role in preventing injuries and enhancing overall workout performance. Understanding how to execute these components properly can help you prepare your body for strenuous activity and aid in recovery afterward.

Warm-ups are designed to gradually prepare your body for exercise by increasing heart rate, blood flow, and muscle temperature. This preparation helps improve muscle elasticity, reducing the risk of strains and other injuries. A good warm-up should last about 5 to 10 minutes and involve light aerobic activities that mimic the movements of the workout. For instance, if you plan a leg workout, your warm-up could include light jogging or cycling followed by dynamic stretches such as leg swings and walking lunges. These activities help activate the muscles you will use during your session.

Incorporating dynamic stretching into your warm-up is beneficial. It involves moving parts of your body and gradually increasing reach, speed of movement, or both. This type of stretching is preferable to static stretching before a workout because it helps improve functional range of motion and performance.

Cool-downs, however, help your body transition back to rest gradually. After a vigorous workout, abruptly stopping can cause lightheadedness or palpitations as blood pools in the large muscles of the legs instead of returning to the heart and brain. A cool-down session might last about 5 to 10 minutes and typically involves gradually reducing the workout intensity. For example, if you were running, you would slow down to jog and walk.

Following the light aerobic activity, cool-downs should include static stretching. This is where you stretch and hold a single position for up to 30 seconds, helping to relax the muscles, improve flexibility, and reduce muscle soreness. Focus on stretching major muscle groups involved in the workout, and pay particular attention to any areas of tightness or discomfort.

Implementing effective warm-ups and cool-downs not only minimizes the risk of injury but also enhances the effectiveness of your workouts and aids in quicker muscle recovery. These practices are integral to any training session and should not be skipped if you want to maintain long-term fitness and health.

Incorporating flexibility work to prevent injuries

Incorporating flexibility work into your training routine is an effective way to prevent injuries and improve overall strength training performance. Flexibility exercises increase the range of motion in your joints, reduce muscle tension, and help your body move more efficiently during everyday activities and intense workouts.

Regular flexibility training, such as stretching, yoga, or Pilates, allows muscles to work most effectively. It prevents the muscles from becoming too tight and shortened, leading to muscle imbalances and increased susceptibility to tearing.

Static stretching is one of the most common methods to enhance flexibility. It involves elongating a muscle to its furthest point and holding that position for 20 to 30 seconds. While this type of stretching is beneficial post-workout when the muscles are warm, dynamic stretching, which involves moving parts of your body and gradually increasing reach, speed, or both, is more beneficial before workouts. Dynamic stretches prepare the body for the movements it will perform during the session, thus reducing the risk of injuries from movements that exceed the muscles' current range.

Yoga is another excellent way to improve flexibility. It combines deep breathing with a series of positions that stretch and strengthen the body. This enhances flexibility and improves balance and core strength, which are vital for maintaining proper posture and alignment during other forms of exercise.

Pilates also focuses on control and precision, with exercises that promote muscle lengthening. It can be especially beneficial in building core strength, improving posture, and increasing flexibility in the muscles of the back and limbs.

In addition to preventing injuries, flexibility work can aid muscle recovery and reduce soreness after workouts. Improving blood flow to the muscles: These exercises help speed recovery and decrease the time needed for muscles to heal between training sessions.

Consider dedicating a specific time for each training session to integrate flexibility work effectively. A common approach is to perform dynamic stretches as part of the warm-up and then finish with static stretches during the cool-down. Alternatively, dedicating entire sessions to yoga or Pilates can provide a deep focus on flexibility, balance, and core strength.

Making flexibility a consistent part of your strength training regimen helps keep your muscles and joints in good working order and enhances your overall athletic performance.

Strategies to train around existing injuries

Training around existing injuries requires a thoughtful and cautious approach to ensure the body stays active without worsening the injury. The first and most crucial step is to talk to a healthcare professional, such as a physiotherapist or doctor, before continuing or adjusting your workouts. They can help you understand the limits of your injury and guide you on what movements to avoid and what activities are still safe.

Once you have medical advice, you can begin to modify your workouts. The goal should be to stay active without stressing the injured area. For example, if you have an injury in your lower body, like a knee or ankle issue, you might shift your focus to upper-body exercises or gentle core work that doesn't require leg involvement. On the other hand, if the injury is in your shoulder or wrist, focusing on leg strength or gentle aerobic activities may be a better option.

Choosing low-impact movements can also be helpful when working around injuries. Exercises like walking, cycling on a stationary bike, or swimming are often easier on the joints and can keep you moving without placing unnecessary pressure on sensitive areas. You should also consider using lighter weights or exercises with resistance bands, offering more control and less strain.

Another good strategy is to strengthen the muscles surrounding the injury, as long as it doesn't cause pain. Strengthening supporting muscles can provide added stability and support to the injured area, potentially speeding up the healing process. That said, always move carefully and stop any exercise that causes discomfort or pain.

Paying attention to how your body feels during and after your workouts is very important. If something doesn't feel right, it probably isn't. Avoid pushing through sharp or unusual pain, which can worsen the injury or delay healing. Even if an exercise used to feel easy or familiar, an injury changes how your body moves and reacts, so be patient and flexible with your progress.

Proper form and attention to technique are even more critical when recovering from an injury. If needed, use equipment that supports the injured area, like a brace or wrap, and take your time to perform each movement carefully. It's also helpful to give your body more time to rest between sessions and prioritize sleep and good nutrition, as these factors help with healing and overall recovery.

Staying active during injury recovery can be possible and helpful as long as the approach is gentle, safe, and guided by your body's signals. With patience and proper adjustments, you can continue building strength and maintaining fitness without risking your recovery.

CHAPTER 13

Incorporating Cardio and Flexibility

While strength training builds muscle, improves bone density, and enhances overall power, it's equally important to include cardio and flexibility work as part of a well-rounded fitness routine. Cardiovascular exercise supports heart health, boosts endurance, and helps with fat loss, while flexibility training improves mobility, prevents injury, and supports recovery. Together, they complement your strength training efforts, allowing your body to move better, recover faster, and perform more efficiently in daily life. In this chapter, we'll explore how to find the right balance between strength, cardio, and flexibility to create a routine that supports both your short-term progress and long-term health.

Balancing strength training with cardiovascular health

Balancing strength training with cardiovascular exercise is essential for maintaining overall health and achieving a well-rounded fitness routine. While strength training focuses on building muscle, increasing metabolism, and supporting bone health, cardiovascular workouts help improve heart and lung function, increase endurance, and assist in managing weight. Finding the right balance between the two ensures your body remains strong, agile, and efficient in handling both physical activity and daily life demands.

It's not about choosing one over the other but rather understanding how they work together. Strength training helps shape and support your body, while cardio keeps your heart strong and your circulation efficient. For women who are aiming to build lean muscle and burn fat, combining these two forms of exercise can be especially effective. Strength training boosts metabolism by increasing muscle mass, which in turn helps you burn more calories even when at rest. Cardio supports fat loss by burning calories during the workout and improving the body's ability to use oxygen.

You don't need to spend hours doing cardio to see results. Short, consistent sessions throughout the week can make a big difference. This could mean brisk walking, cycling, swimming, or even dancing for 20 to 30 minutes a few times a week. On days when you're doing strength training, cardio can be kept light, perhaps as a warm-up or cool-down. On other days, a full cardio session can help improve endurance and support recovery by increasing blood flow to the muscles.

It's also helpful to listen to your body and adjust your routine based on how you feel. Some weeks you might need more recovery and lighter cardio, while other times you may feel energized and ready for more. The key is to create a schedule that fits your lifestyle, supports your goals, and leaves you feeling strong and refreshed, not burned out.

Including both strength training and cardiovascular exercise in your routine, you'll not only improve your fitness but also support your heart, boost your energy levels, and feel better both physically and mentally. The balance doesn't have to be perfect every day, but over time, combining these elements creates a strong foundation for lasting health.

Benefits of static stretching

Static stretching offers several important benefits, especially when included at the right time in your fitness routine. Unlike dynamic stretching, which involves movement, static stretching means holding a muscle in a lengthened position for a short period, usually around 20 to 30 seconds. It's most effective when done after exercise, during the cool-down phase, when your muscles are already warm and more flexible.

One of the main benefits of static stretching is improved flexibility. Over time, regularly holding stretches helps lengthen the muscles and improve your range of motion. This can make everyday movements feel easier and more comfortable, whether you're reaching, bending, or walking up stairs. Increased flexibility also helps with better posture and muscle balance, which reduces the risk of developing movement-related pain or tightness, especially in the back, neck, and shoulders.

Another advantage of static stretching is how it helps muscles relax after a workout. After strength training or cardio, your muscles may feel tight or tense. Holding a gentle stretch can help signal your body to slow down, bringing your heart rate and breathing back to normal. This transition into recovery not only feels good but can also reduce the chances of post-workout soreness and stiffness.

Static stretching also supports injury prevention. By maintaining flexible and well-balanced muscles, you lower your risk of strains and pulls that can occur when muscles are too tight or imbalanced. For example, stretching the hamstrings, calves, or hip flexors regularly can help prevent common injuries in the legs and lower back, especially for those who sit for long periods or do repetitive movements.

Additionally, static stretching offers mental benefits. The slow, steady nature of these stretches encourages mindfulness and relaxation. Taking a few minutes to stretch after exercise or at the end of the day can provide a calm moment that helps reduce stress and improve your overall sense of well-being.

When done consistently, static stretching helps your body move better, recover faster, and feel more balanced. While it shouldn't replace other parts of your fitness routine, it's a simple and effective way to support your overall flexibility and long-term physical health.

Benefits of dynamic stretching

Dynamic stretching offers a wide range of benefits, especially when used before a workout to prepare the body for movement. Unlike static stretching, which involves holding a stretch in one position, dynamic stretching involves controlled, active movements that gently take your muscles and joints through their full range of motion. This type of stretching helps to increase blood flow, raise body temperature, and activate the nervous system, all of which help prepare the body for physical activity.

One of the biggest advantages of dynamic stretching is that it wakes up the muscles you're about to use. By mimicking the movements of your upcoming workout, dynamic stretches help improve muscle coordination and reaction time. For example, doing leg swings before a leg workout or arm circles before an upper body routine helps warm up those specific muscle groups and increases joint mobility. This preparation makes your body more responsive and ready for the physical demands of your training.

Dynamic stretching also reduces the risk of injury by gently loosening up the muscles and tendons without forcing them into uncomfortable positions. Since it keeps your body in motion, it helps maintain momentum and gradually increases flexibility without the sudden tension that can sometimes happen with static stretching when muscles are still cold.

Another benefit is improved athletic performance. When your muscles are warm and fully prepared for movement, you're more likely to move with power, speed, and control. Dynamic stretching can enhance your ability to lift weights with better form or perform cardio with more efficiency, making your workouts more productive and safe.

This type of stretching can also be mentally stimulating. The movement involved requires focus and coordination, which helps your mind transition into an active state. This mental preparation can be especially helpful if you're feeling sluggish or distracted before a workout.

In short, dynamic stretching is an important part of your warm-up routine. It helps your body move more easily, reduces the risk of injury, and prepares both your muscles and your mind for the activity ahead. Including a few minutes of dynamic movement before every workout can lead to better performance and a safer, more effective training session.

Creating a balanced weekly training schedule

Creating a balanced weekly training schedule is important for making steady progress, avoiding burnout, and giving your body the recovery time it needs to stay strong and healthy. A good schedule includes a mix of strength training, cardio, flexibility work, and rest. Each element plays a role in building a well-rounded, sustainable fitness routine that supports both short-term goals and long-term health.

The key is to spread out different types of workouts across the week so your body has time to recover between intense sessions. For example, if you plan to strength train three times a week, it's helpful to alternate training days with cardio or flexibility-focused activities. You might lift weights on Monday, Wednesday, and Friday, and go for a brisk walk, bike ride, or light jog on Tuesday and Thursday. This keeps you active throughout the week without overloading the same muscle groups every day.

Including flexibility work like stretching, yoga, or Pilates at least two or three times a week can help reduce muscle tension, improve mobility, and prevent injuries. These sessions don't have to be long—just 15 to 20 minutes after a workout or on a recovery day can make a noticeable difference over time.

It's also important to have at least one full rest day each week, where you give your muscles and nervous system a break from structured exercise. On this day, you can still be lightly active by doing things like gentle walking or simply going about your daily routine without a workout. Rest is when your body repairs and rebuilds, which is essential for gaining strength and avoiding fatigue.

Sticking to a regular training schedule not only keeps you consistent but also makes it easier to track progress and build habits. If you're new to exercising, starting with three to four sessions per week and gradually increasing as your fitness improves is a smart approach. Over time, you'll learn what combination of workouts leaves you feeling energized, motivated, and physically balanced.

A well-structured weekly plan doesn't have to be perfect, but it should fit your lifestyle, respect your energy levels, and support your goals. Being flexible with your schedule and listening to your body will help you stay committed and enjoy the benefits of training week after week.

CHAPTER 14

Tracking Progress and Adjusting Your Plan

Keeping track of your progress is one of the most powerful ways to stay motivated and ensure your strength training efforts genuinely work for you. It helps you see how far you've come, what's working, and what might need to change. This chapter focuses on simple, practical ways to monitor your workouts, measure your results, and use that information to make intelligent adjustments to your training plan. Whether your goal is to get stronger, leaner, or feel better, learning to track your progress and tweak your routine as needed will help you stay on the right path and continue moving forward confidently.

Why and how to log your workouts

Logging your workouts is one of the easiest and most effective ways to stay consistent and make real progress in your strength training journey. When you write down what you did during each session, you create a clear picture of your efforts over time. This can be incredibly motivating, especially when you feel stuck or unsure if you're improving. Looking back at past workouts lets you see how much stronger you've become, how much weight you've added, or how your endurance has increased. Even minor improvements, like doing one extra repetition or lifting a slightly heavier dumbbell, are easier to notice and celebrate when recorded.

A workout log also helps you stay organized. Instead of trying to remember how many sets or reps you did last week, you can check your notes. This makes it easier to follow a structured plan and avoid repeating the same workouts repeatedly without progression. Logging your workouts helps prevent plateaus by encouraging you to challenge yourself in a controlled and safe way, whether by adding weight, adjusting reps, or trying a new exercise.

There are many simple ways to log your workouts. You can use a notebook, a calendar, a phone app, or even a spreadsheet. What matters most is that you record the basics: the exercises you did, the number of sets and reps, the amount of weight used, and how you felt during the workout. Some people also like to include notes about energy levels, sleep, or mood, which can help spot patterns and understand what might affect their performance.

Writing things down doesn't need to be complicated or time-consuming. A few lines after each session are enough to keep track of your progress and give you valuable feedback. Over time, these records become helpful tools that guide your training, hold you accountable, and show you what's working. More importantly, it turns your workouts into part of a bigger story that shows your commitment, growth, and ability to stick with your goals, even when it feels hard.

Different methods to measure progress

Measuring your progress in strength training isn't just about stepping on a scale. There are many ways to see how far you've come, and using a mix of methods gives a more precise and complete picture of your results. One of the most apparent signs of progress is getting stronger. If you're lifting heavier weights now than you were a few weeks or months ago, that's a clear indicator that your muscles are growing and adapting. Tracking how much weight you lift, how many reps you can do, or how many sets you complete can show steady improvement, even when the physical changes aren't immediately visible.

Another way to measure progress is through body changes. This might include noticing your clothes fitting differently, seeing more muscle definition in the mirror, or taking measurements of your waist, hips, arms, or thighs. Sometimes, the scale doesn't change much, especially when building muscle and losing fat simultaneously. That's why it can be helpful to take photos every few weeks. Comparing these side by side can show changes that might not be obvious daily.

You can also track your energy levels, mood, and feelings during workouts. If you find that you're less tired, more focused, and recovering faster, these are all signs your body is getting fitter. Improved sleep, less soreness, and better stamina during exercise all point toward progress, even if you don't see it right away on the outside.

Paying attention to your form and control during exercises is another subtle but essential way to notice improvement. Being able to perform movements with better posture, smoother motion, and more confidence means your strength, coordination, and muscle awareness are growing.

Some people also like to use fitness tests or challenges every few weeks, like seeing how many squats or push-ups they can do in a minute, how long they can hold a plank, or how fast they can walk or jog a certain distance. These are practical ways to see functional gains and track endurance or strength increases over time.

Ultimately, the best method for measuring progress is the one that feels right for you. Whether through numbers, how you look and feel, or how you move, staying aware of your improvements keeps you motivated and helps you stay committed to your training goals.

Using feedback to adjust your training plan

Using feedback to adjust your training plan is an innovative and necessary part of making progress. Your body is always telling you how you feel during and after a workout, how much energy you have, how sore you are, how quickly you recover, and whether or not you're seeing the results you expected. Paying attention to this feedback helps you know when to push harder, slow down, or change your routine to keep moving forward.

If you're feeling stronger, lifting more weight, or finishing workouts with better form and less effort, that's a sign your plan is working, and you might be ready to increase the challenge. This could mean adding weight, doing extra sets or reps, or trying advanced exercises. On the other hand, if you're constantly tired, not sleeping well, or feeling sore for days after each session, it might be a sign you're overtraining or not recovering enough. In that case, it could scale back, add a rest day, or focus on lighter movement and recovery for a while.

Progress might also slow down if you're doing the same workouts repeatedly without any change. If your body has adapted to the routine and you do not see improvements, it may be time to switch up your exercises, try a different training split, or change the order of your workouts. Sometimes, even small changes can spark new growth and make your training feel fresh again.

Listening to your mindset is also essential. If you're feeling bored, frustrated, or unmotivated, that's feedback too. Changing the type of workouts you do, training with a friend, or setting new short-term goals can help bring your motivation back. Fitness is not just physical—it's mental, too, and adjusting your plan to keep things enjoyable can make a big difference in sticking with it.

Tracking progress through workout logs, photos, measurements, or how your clothes fit helps you make these adjustments more clearly. Instead of guessing what's working, you'll have evidence to guide your decisions.

The key is to stay flexible and open to change. Your training plan doesn't have to be perfect—it just has to keep evolving with you. As your goals, lifestyle, and body change, your workouts should too. Making small, thoughtful changes based on what your body tells you can lead to steady, long-term progress and a more enjoyable fitness journey.

Staying adaptable to ongoing changes

Staying adaptable to ongoing changes is one of the most essential parts of building a long-term, successful strength training routine. Life doesn't always go as planned—schedules shift, energy levels fluctuate, responsibilities change, and your body goes through different phases. What works perfectly for you one month might not fit your lifestyle or needs the next. That's why flexibility in your mindset and training plan is so valuable.

Instead of viewing your workout plan as something rigid that must be followed no matter what, it helps to see it as a guide that can be adjusted based on how you feel and what's happening in your life. You might feel strong and energized for weeks, ready to push your limits. Other times, you might be dealing with stress, lack of sleep, or a busy schedule, and your workouts need to shift to match your current state. Adapting doesn't mean you're giving up — you're listening to your body and being smart about your training.

There may also be times when your goals change. You may start wanting to build muscle but later focus more on endurance, flexibility, or weight management. Your training plan can and should shift with those changes. You're not stuck doing the same exercises or following the same routine forever. Strength training offers endless variety, and being open to trying new things can keep your workouts fresh, enjoyable, and aligned with your goals.

Physical changes also come into play. As your body gets more substantial and experienced, you'll need to challenge it in new ways. As you age, recover from injury, or move through different stages of life, your body might need more rest, slower progression, or a different type of movement altogether. Paying attention to your feelings and responding with minor, thoughtful adjustments can help you stay consistent while honoring your body's needs.

Being adaptable also means letting go of perfection. Missing a workout or needing to cut a session short doesn't mean you've failed. Progress is not always linear. It's about showing up however you can, adjusting your plan when needed, and moving forward at your own pace.

The people who stick with training long-term aren't the ones who never miss a session — they're the ones who keep going, even when things don't go as planned. By staying adaptable and permitting yourself to adjust, you build a routine that works not just for now but for the long run.

CHAPTER 15

Every journey is different, and the most powerful proof of what strength training can do comes from the real stories of women who've lived it. This chapter celebrates those stories—the quiet victories, the bold transformations, and the everyday moments of courage that often go unnoticed. Whether it's gaining confidence, overcoming setbacks, building a healthier body, or simply showing up day after day, these women remind us that strength isn't just physical. It's in their mindset, resilience, and ability to keep going even when it's hard. Through their experiences, you'll find inspiration, motivation, and maybe even a reflection of your path.

Transformations through strength training

Transformations through strength training go far beyond physical appearance. For many women, the most meaningful changes happen from the inside out. It starts with that first workout—maybe it feels awkward, unfamiliar, even intimidating—but over time, something shifts. Muscles grow stronger, yes, but so does self-belief. Tasks that once felt heavy, like carrying groceries or climbing stairs, suddenly become more effortless. That sense of capability begins to spill over into everyday life.

For some women, strength training has been the key to reclaiming their bodies after years of feeling disconnected. Others have used it to rebuild after illness, injury, or emotional struggles. In each case, the gym becomes more than just a place to work out. It becomes a space for growth, healing, and proving to themselves what they're truly capable of.

There are stories of women who walked in unsure of what they could do and left lifting weights they never imagined they'd touch. Stories of women who didn't just lose weight or build muscle but gained energy, confidence, and a more profound respect for their bodies. Some were motivated by health scares, others by a desire to set an example for their children, and many wanted to feel strong and in control again.

These transformations don't always come quickly. They happen through consistency, patience, and showing up on good days and bad. There are setbacks and plateaus, but there are also breakthroughs—moments when something just clicks, progress becomes obvious, and hard work starts to show not just in the mirror but in posture, mood, and how someone carries themselves.

What makes these stories powerful isn't perfection—it's perseverance. These are real women with real lives who made time for themselves and discovered their strength one step, one rep, and one day at a time. Their experiences prove that strength training isn't just about fitness. It's about discovering what you're made of and realizing you're capable of more than you thought.

Overcoming challenges and setbacks

Overcoming challenges and setbacks is a part of every strength training journey, and for many women, it's where the most potent growth happens. Progress is rarely smooth or predictable. There are moments of frustration, times when motivation dips, and days when the body doesn't cooperate. Life gets busy, injuries happen, confidence wavers, and sometimes everything works against you. But these moments test your commitment and reveal your inner strength.

Some women initially face doubts—questions about whether they belong in a gym, are strong enough, or are doing things the right way. Others deal with external pressures, like unsupportive environments or a lack of time and resources. Many have to fight through their self-criticism, comparing themselves to others or focusing too much on what they haven't achieved yet.

Then, physical setbacks, like injuries or health issues, force a pause. These moments can be discouraging, especially when progress seems to slip away. But what often happens is that women come back even more determined. They learn to train smarter, listen more closely to their bodies, and rebuild at a pace that works for them. The pause becomes a turning point, not an end.

Mental and emotional challenges also come into play. Some days feel heavier than others, and the weight on your shoulders isn't just the barbell. But choosing to show up anyway—even if the workout is shorter, lighter, or slower—is a form of strength. It's about honoring the process, not just the results.

What's inspiring is how many women push through these hard seasons and come out physically and mentally stronger. They adapt, learn, and remind themselves that progress is still happening, even when it's not visible. These experiences build resilience, patience, and trust in the journey.

Every setback offers a chance to grow in a new way. Every challenge overcome adds to the quiet strength that builds with every lift, every stretch, and every choice to keep going. The road isn't always easy, but it's always worth it—and these stories prove just how powerful and capable women are, even when the path is full of obstacles.

Achievements in competitive arenas

Achievements in competitive arenas show just how far strength training can take women—in physical ability, confidence, discipline, and self-belief. For many, stepping into a competitive space is a bold decision. It means putting yourself out there, setting ambitious goals, and working with focus and dedication over time. Whether it's powerlifting, bodybuilding, CrossFit, or local fitness competitions, these events are more than just physical tests—they're personal milestones.

Some women start with no intention of competing. They train for health, energy, or to feel better. But as they get stronger and more consistent, their mindset shifts. They begin to see what they're capable of and eventually set their sights on something bigger. Entering a competition, even a small one, becomes a way to challenge themselves, push their limits, and step into a version of themselves they might never have imagined.

For others, competition is a goal from the beginning. They train with structure, measure every rep and meal, and visualize when they step onto a platform or stage. The preparation is intense. It demands long hours, mental focus, and sometimes setbacks. But those moments of struggle often lead to the most rewarding achievements.

Winning isn't the only success. For many, just showing up and competing is a huge accomplishment—especially after overcoming fear, doubt, or obstacles that once felt overwhelming. These achievements represent more than just trophies or rankings. They're proof of commitment, growth, and the courage to do something that once felt impossible.

Competing also connects women with others who share similar passions and goals. It builds a sense of community and support, where victories are celebrated together, and even the tough days are understood and respected. Whether it's lifting a personal best, placing in a competition, or simply crossing the finish line, these moments remind women of their strength and the pride that comes from pursuing something with their whole heart.

These stories from the competitive world are not just about athleticism—they're about transformation, resilience, and the power of setting goals beyond comfort zones. They show that strength training can be more than a routine. For many women, it becomes a path to confidence, connection, and unforgettable achievements.

Daily victories and personal milestones

Daily victories and personal milestones often hold the most meaning, even if they don't come with trophies or public recognition. These are the quiet moments of success in everyday life — the small wins that build up over time and remind women how far they've come. It might be the first time someone lifts a weight they never thought they could. It might be walking upstairs without feeling winded, carrying groceries easily, or waking up without the usual aches and pains. These victories are personal, but they are powerful.

For many women, starting strength training takes courage. Pushing through self-doubt, showing up consistently, learning proper form, and navigating a gym environment can initially feel intimidating. But over time, those early struggles turn into confidence. Lifting becomes less scary, movement becomes more natural, and progress feels within reach. These milestones may seem small to others but are deeply meaningful to the person achieving them.

It's also about emotional strength — learning to trust your body, appreciate it, and speak to yourself with kindness. Some women notice they stand taller, not just physically but mentally. They begin to take up space without apology. They feel more in control, not just during a workout but also in other areas of life.

There are also moments of persistence that deserve celebration. There are days when it would have been easier to skip a workout, but they showed up anyway. Sometimes, progress felt slow, but they didn't give up. Choosing to care for yourself consistently, even when no one else sees it, is an achievement.

These daily victories often go unnoticed by the outside world but are the foundation of long-term transformation. They prove that strength isn't just measured in how much you lift or how fast you run — it's also in the discipline, the patience, and the decision to keep going, one day at a time. Those small milestones add up over the weeks and months, creating a sense of pride and progress that no one can take away. And in the end, it's often these moments that women look back on and realize just how strong they've become.

CHAPTER 16

The Essential 30 - Core Exercises for Every Woman

Strength training doesn't have to be complicated to be effective. With the right set of exercises, you can build a strong, balanced body that supports your everyday movements, improves your posture, and boosts your confidence. This chapter introduces thirty essential exercises that every woman can benefit from—covering all major muscle groups and offering a mix of foundational movements, functional training, and dynamic strength work. Whether you're training at home or in the gym, a beginner or more advanced, these exercises can be adapted to fit your level and goals. Together, they form a powerful toolkit that supports both your health and strength journey, helping you move better, feel stronger, and stay active for life.

Squats

Squats are one of the best exercises for your lower body. They help make your legs, hips, and butt stronger. Squats also work your core and improve balance and posture. This exercise is useful in daily life too—like when you sit, stand, or lift something.

You can start with just your body weight. Later, you can use dumbbells or other weights to make it harder.

How to do a basic bodyweight squat:

- Stand with your feet shoulder-width apart, toes slightly pointed out.
- Keep your chest up and your back straight.
- Tighten your stomach muscles.
- Push your hips back, like you're going to sit on a chair.
- Bend your knees and lower your body slowly.
- Go down until your thighs are flat or as low as you can go.
- Keep your heels on the floor and knees in line with your toes.

- Push through your heels to stand up again.
- Don't lock your knees at the top.
- Repeat the move for as many times as you like.

You can hold your arms out in front to help with balance. If it's hard to go low, use a chair to guide your depth. Once you're comfortable, try harder versions like holding a weight or doing jump squats.

Squats are simple but powerful. They help you move better, feel stronger, and stay fit.

Deadlifts

Deadlifts are a strong, full-body exercise that mainly works your back, legs, and core. They help you build strength in your hamstrings, glutes, lower back, and even your grip. Deadlifts are great for everyday movements like lifting heavy bags, boxes, or even children safely. When done the right way, they can improve posture and make your whole body stronger.

You can start with a light barbell, dumbbells, or even just practice the movement with no weight at all if you're a beginner.

How to do a basic deadlift:

- Stand with your feet hip-width apart and the weight (like a barbell or dumbbells) in front of you.
- Keep your chest up, shoulders back, and back straight.
- Bend at your hips and knees to lower your hands down to the weight.
- Grab the weight with both hands and keep your arms straight.
- Tighten your core and push through your heels to stand up.
- As you lift, keep the weight close to your legs and your back flat.
- Stand tall at the top, but don't lean back or lock your knees.
- Lower the weight slowly by bending your hips and knees, returning to the starting position.
- Repeat as needed, keeping control and good form.

Always move slowly and with focus. Don't round your back. If you're unsure about your form, use a mirror or ask a trainer to check. Once you get stronger and more confident, you can try harder deadlift styles like Romanian or sumo deadlifts.

Deadlifts are one of the best moves to build real-life strength. Done correctly, they'll help you lift better, move better, and feel stronger all over.

Lunges

Lunges are a great lower-body exercise that strengthens your legs, hips, and glutes. They also help improve balance, coordination, and flexibility. Because lunges work one leg at a time, they can fix muscle imbalances and make both legs equally strong. They're simple, need no equipment, and can be done anywhere.

How to do a basic bodyweight lunge:

- Stand up straight with your feet hip-width apart.
- Take a big step forward with one leg.
- Lower your body by bending both knees.
- Your front thigh should be parallel to the floor, and your back knee should hover just above the ground.
- Keep your chest up, back straight, and your front knee in line with your ankle.
- Push through your front heel to return to the starting position.
- Switch legs and repeat.

You can hold dumbbells at your sides to make the exercise harder once you feel confident with your form. You can also try walking lunges or reverse lunges to keep things interesting.

Lunges help make your legs stronger, improve your balance, and prepare your body for real-life movements like climbing stairs or bending down safely. They're easy to learn and super effective when done regularly.

Bench Press

Bench press is a classic upper-body strength exercise that mainly works your chest, shoulders, and triceps. It helps build pushing power and muscle in the upper body, which is useful for daily tasks like pushing doors, lifting objects, or even getting up from the floor. You can do it with a barbell or dumbbells, either on a flat bench or with slight angles to target different parts of the chest.

How to do a basic bench press with a barbell:

- Lie flat on a bench with your eyes under the bar.
- Place your feet flat on the floor and keep your back slightly arched.
- Grab the bar with both hands, a little wider than shoulder-width apart.
- Lift the bar off the rack and hold it above your chest with straight arms.
- Slowly lower the bar down to the middle of your chest.
- Keep your elbows at about a 45-degree angle from your body.
- Push the bar back up until your arms are straight again.

- Repeat for your desired number of reps, then carefully return the bar to the rack.

Start with light weight to learn good form. If you're using heavy weights, always have a spotter to help for safety. You can also do bench presses with dumbbells if you don't have a barbell.

The bench press builds strength and muscle in your upper body, making you stronger for both workouts and everyday tasks. With proper form and regular practice, it's a great addition to your strength training routine.

Overhead Press

Overhead press is a powerful upper-body exercise that mainly works your shoulders, along with your triceps and upper chest. It also engages your core and helps improve posture and overall upper-body strength. This move trains you to push weight above your head, which is useful in daily life when reaching for or lifting things overhead.

How to do a basic overhead press with dumbbells:

- Stand tall with your feet shoulder-width apart.
- Hold a dumbbell in each hand at shoulder level, palms facing forward.
- Keep your chest up, back straight, and core tight.
- Press the dumbbells straight up over your head until your arms are fully extended.
- Pause briefly at the top, without locking your elbows.
- Slowly lower the dumbbells back to shoulder level.
- Repeat for your desired number of reps.

You can also do this exercise seated for more back support. If using a barbell, use a similar motion but with both hands on the bar at shoulder-width apart.

Start with light weights to learn the movement, and focus on keeping your core engaged so your lower back doesn't arch. The overhead press is great for building strength in your shoulders and arms, helping you move better and lift more with confidence.

Pull-ups

Pull-ups are one of the best bodyweight exercises for building upper-body strength. They mainly work your back muscles, especially the lats, and also target your biceps, shoulders, and core. Doing pull-ups can improve posture, grip strength, and overall pulling power, which helps with daily movements like climbing, lifting, and carrying heavy objects.

How to do a basic pull-up:

- Grab a pull-up bar with your hands slightly wider than shoulder-width apart, palms facing away from you.
- Hang from the bar with your arms fully extended and your legs straight or slightly bent.
- Tighten your core and pull your chest up toward the bar by bending your elbows and squeezing your shoulder blades together.
- Continue pulling until your chin is above the bar.
- Lower yourself slowly and with control back to the starting position.
- Repeat for as many reps as you can.

Pull-ups are challenging, especially for beginners. If you're not able to do one yet, you can start with assisted pull-ups using a resistance band or a machine. You can also try negative pull-ups by jumping up to the top position and slowly lowering yourself down.

With practice, pull-ups build strong, lean muscles and give you a real sense of accomplishment. They're tough, but worth the effort—and every rep brings you closer to feeling stronger and more capable.

Rows

Rows are a great exercise for building a strong back and improving posture. They mainly target the upper and middle back muscles, including the lats, rhomboids, and traps, and they also work the biceps and shoulders. Rows help balance the body, especially if you're doing a lot of pushing exercises like bench presses or push-ups. A strong back is key for everyday tasks like pulling, lifting, and carrying.

How to do a basic bent-over dumbbell row:

- Hold a dumbbell in each hand with your palms facing your body.
- Stand with your feet hip-width apart and bend your knees slightly.
- Hinge at your hips and lean your torso forward while keeping your back flat and core tight.
- Let your arms hang straight down under your shoulders.
- Pull the dumbbells up toward your waist, squeezing your shoulder blades together.
- Keep your elbows close to your sides.
- Lower the dumbbells slowly back to the starting position.
- Repeat for the desired number of reps.

You can also do rows with a barbell, resistance band, or cable machine. If you're new to rows, start with light weights and focus on form.

Rows are an important part of any balanced workout routine. They build back strength, help improve your posture, and protect your shoulders from injury. Done regularly and with proper form, rows can make you feel stronger and more stable in everyday movement.

Plank Variations

Plank variations are excellent exercises for building core strength, improving stability, and supporting better posture. While a basic plank works your abs, back, and shoulders, changing the position or movement can make the exercise more challenging and target different muscles. Plank variations can be done anywhere with no equipment, making them perfect for home workouts.

How to do a basic forearm plank:

- Start by lying face down on the floor.
- Place your forearms on the ground, elbows under your shoulders.
- Lift your body up so that you're resting on your forearms and toes.
- Keep your body in a straight line from head to heels.
- Tighten your core and avoid letting your hips drop or rise too high.
- Hold the position for as long as you can with good form.

Once you're comfortable with the basic plank, you can try these simple variations:

- **Side plank:** Turn onto one forearm and stack your feet, lifting your hips to work the obliques (side abs).
- **Plank with shoulder taps:** From a high plank, tap each shoulder with the opposite hand while keeping your hips steady.
- **Plank with leg lifts:** In a forearm or high plank, lift one leg at a time to challenge your core and glutes.
- **Walking plank:** Move from a forearm plank to a high plank and back down, alternating arms.

Plank variations are great because they train your core in different ways while also working your arms, shoulders, and legs. Adding a few of these to your workout helps build full-body control and stability, making all your other movements stronger and safer.

Leg Press

Leg press is a popular strength training exercise that targets your lower body, especially the quadriceps, hamstrings, and glutes. It's usually done on a leg press machine, which allows you to push weight away from your body using your legs while keeping your back supported. This makes it a great option for beginners or those who want to train their legs without putting too much pressure on their lower back.

How to do a basic leg press:

- Sit on the leg press machine and place your feet flat on the platform, about shoulder-width apart.
- Make sure your knees are in line with your toes and not locked.
- Keep your back and head pressed against the seat and grab the handles for support.
- Slowly push the platform away from you by straightening your legs.
- Stop just before locking your knees at the top.
- Lower the platform by bending your knees until they're at about a 90-degree angle.
- Push through your heels to return to the starting position.
- Repeat for the desired number of reps.

Start with a light weight to learn proper form and avoid injury. Keep the movement smooth and controlled, and don't rush through the reps. Over time, you can increase the weight as your leg strength improves.

The leg press is a safe and effective way to build strong legs and glutes. It's especially helpful if you're not yet comfortable with squats or if you want to add extra lower-body training to your routine.

Dumbbell Curls

Dumbbell curls are a simple and effective exercise to build strength in your arms, especially the biceps. They also help improve grip and support other upper-body movements like pulling and lifting. This exercise can be done standing or sitting and doesn't require a lot of space or equipment—just a pair of dumbbells.

How to do a basic dumbbell curl:

- Stand tall with your feet shoulder-width apart.
- Hold a dumbbell in each hand with your arms down by your sides and your palms facing forward.
- Keep your elbows close to your body and your back straight.
- Slowly bend your elbows to lift the dumbbells toward your shoulders.
- Squeeze your biceps at the top of the movement.
- Lower the dumbbells back down with control to the starting position.
- Repeat for the desired number of reps.

Make sure not to swing your body or use momentum. Focus on using your arms to lift the weight. Start with a light pair of dumbbells and increase the weight as you get stronger.

Dumbbell curls are great for building toned, strong arms and improving everyday tasks that involve lifting or carrying. When done regularly and with good form, they can make a big difference in your upper-body strength.

Tricep Dips

Tricep dips are a bodyweight exercise that target the triceps—the muscles on the back of your upper arms. They also work your shoulders and chest and are great for building upper body strength. Tricep dips can be done almost anywhere using a sturdy chair, bench, or even stairs.

How to do a basic tricep dip using a chair or bench:

- Sit on the edge of a sturdy chair or bench with your hands next to your hips, fingers pointing forward.
- Slide your hips off the edge so your weight is supported by your hands, and keep your feet flat on the floor with your knees bent.
- Slowly bend your elbows and lower your body straight down until your elbows are at about a 90-degree angle.
- Keep your back close to the chair and your chest lifted.
- Press through your hands to straighten your arms and lift your body back up to the starting position.
- Repeat for the desired number of reps.

Keep the movement controlled and avoid letting your shoulders shrug. As you get stronger, you can make it harder by straightening your legs or placing your feet on another bench.

Tricep dips are a simple and effective way to tone the back of your arms and build strength using just your body weight. With regular practice, they can help improve your pushing power and make your arms feel firmer and more capable.

Shoulder Shrugs

Shoulder shrugs are a simple yet powerful exercise that targets the trapezius muscles, which run from the back of your neck across your shoulders and upper back. Strengthening these muscles helps improve posture, reduce neck tension, and support other upper-body movements like lifting and carrying.

How to do basic shoulder shrugs with dumbbells:

- Stand tall with your feet shoulder-width apart.
- Hold a dumbbell in each hand with your arms relaxed by your sides and palms facing your body.
- Keep your back straight and your core engaged.
- Slowly lift your shoulders straight up toward your ears, as if you're saying "I don't know."
- Hold the top position for a second and squeeze your shoulder muscles.
- Lower your shoulders back down in a controlled way.
- Repeat for the desired number of reps.

Avoid rolling your shoulders forward or backward—just move them straight up and down. Use light to moderate weights at first, and focus on using your muscles rather than momentum.

Shoulder shrugs are quick, easy to learn, and very effective for strengthening your upper back and shoulders. When added to your regular routine, they can help you feel more upright, reduce tightness, and support a strong, balanced upper body.

Chest Fly

Chest fly is a great exercise for targeting the chest muscles, especially the pectorals. It also works the shoulders and helps stretch and open up the chest area. This move is usually done lying on a flat bench with dumbbells, but it can also be done on the floor or with a stability ball. Chest fly exercises help improve upper body strength and can make pushing movements easier in daily life.

How to do a basic chest fly with dumbbells:

- Lie flat on a bench with a dumbbell in each hand.
- Hold the dumbbells above your chest with your arms extended but elbows slightly bent.
- Keep your feet flat on the floor and your back pressed gently into the bench.
- Slowly open your arms wide out to the sides in a wide arc, keeping that slight bend in your elbows.
- Lower the dumbbells until they are level with your chest or slightly below.
- Squeeze your chest muscles and bring the dumbbells back up to the starting position using the same arc.
- Repeat for the desired number of reps.
- Move slowly and with control—don't let the dumbbells drop quickly. Keep your shoulders relaxed and avoid locking your elbows.

Chest fly is excellent for shaping and strengthening the chest. When done with good form and light to moderate weights, it helps you build muscle while improving flexibility in your upper body.

Leg Raises

Leg raises are a simple and effective exercise that mainly targets your lower abdominal muscles. They also help strengthen your hip flexors and improve core control and stability. You don't need any equipment for this exercise—just a mat or a soft surface to lie on—making it perfect for home workouts.

How to do basic leg raises:

- Lie flat on your back with your legs straight and your arms resting at your sides.
- Keep your legs together and your feet flexed or relaxed.
- Slowly lift both legs off the ground, keeping them straight, until they form a 90-degree angle with your body or as high as you can go comfortably.
- Pause briefly at the top.
- Lower your legs slowly and with control back down toward the floor, but don't let them touch the ground.
- Repeat for the desired number of reps.

Keep your lower back pressed gently into the floor throughout the movement. If you feel strain in your lower back, place your hands under your hips for extra support or bend your knees slightly during the exercise.

Leg raises help tighten and tone your lower abs, improve core strength, and support better balance and posture. When done consistently with good form, they're a great addition to any full-body or ab-focused workout.

Kettlebell Swings

Kettlebell swings are a powerful full-body exercise that mainly targets your hips, glutes, hamstrings, and core. They also get your heart rate up, making them great for both strength and cardio. This movement teaches you how to use your hips for explosive power, which can improve your athletic performance and help with daily tasks like lifting and bending.

How to do a basic kettlebell swing:

- Stand with your feet shoulder-width apart and the kettlebell on the floor in front of you.
- Bend your knees slightly, hinge at your hips, and grab the kettlebell with both hands.
- Swing the kettlebell back between your legs while keeping your back flat and your core tight.

- Push through your hips to drive the kettlebell forward and up to chest level. Your arms should be relaxed, and the power should come from your hips—not your shoulders.
- Let the kettlebell swing back down between your legs and repeat the motion.

Keep your movements controlled and focus on good form. Don't squat—hinge at your hips. Start with a light kettlebell until you feel confident, then increase the weight gradually.

Kettlebell swings are a great way to build strength, burn calories, and improve endurance. They're fast, fun, and very effective when done correctly.

Barbell Snatch

Barbell snatch is an advanced full-body exercise that builds explosive power, coordination, balance, and strength. It mainly targets the legs, back, shoulders, and core, and is often used in Olympic weightlifting and athletic training. The goal is to lift a barbell from the floor to overhead in one smooth, quick motion.

How to do a basic barbell snatch (simplified version for beginners):

- Stand with your feet shoulder-width apart and the barbell on the floor in front of you.
- Grab the bar with a wide grip, palms facing down, and keep your chest up and back straight.
- Lower your hips and tighten your core, getting into a strong starting position.
- Begin by pulling the bar off the floor using your legs and hips, keeping it close to your body.
- As the bar passes your knees, explode upward by extending your hips and shrugging your shoulders.
- Drop under the bar quickly and catch it overhead with your arms fully extended and your feet in a slight squat.
- Stand up fully with the bar overhead to complete the movement.

The barbell snatch requires practice, proper form, and sometimes coaching to perform safely. Start with a PVC pipe or a very light bar to learn the movement before adding weight.

This lift is challenging but highly rewarding. It builds strength, speed, and body control, making it one of the most dynamic exercises in any advanced training program.

Clean and Jerk

Clean and jerk is a powerful, full-body Olympic weightlifting movement that combines two separate phases: lifting the barbell to your shoulders (the clean), and then pushing it overhead (the jerk). It builds explosive strength, coordination, speed, and stability, and it targets major muscle groups including your legs, back, shoulders, arms, and core.

How to do a basic clean and jerk (beginner-friendly steps):

- Stand with your feet shoulder-width apart and the barbell on the floor in front of you.
- Grab the bar with a shoulder-width grip, palms facing down, and keep your back straight and chest up.
- Start the clean by driving through your legs to lift the bar off the floor, keeping it close to your body.
- As the bar passes your knees, explode upward by extending your hips and shrugging your shoulders.
- Drop under the bar and catch it at your shoulders in a front squat position with elbows pointing forward.
- Stand up straight to complete the clean part of the lift.
- For the jerk, bend your knees slightly, then push through your legs to drive the bar overhead.
- Catch the bar with your arms fully extended, either by jumping into a split stance or keeping your feet even.
- Bring your feet back together under control and stand tall with the bar overhead.
- Lower the bar safely to the ground.

The clean and jerk is a technical movement and should be practiced with light weight at first. It's helpful to break it down into parts and work with a coach or experienced lifter to learn proper form.

When done correctly, this lift develops serious power and full-body strength. It's one of the most athletic movements in weightlifting and offers huge benefits for performance and fitness.

Hip Thrusts

Hip thrusts are a highly effective exercise for building strong glutes, hamstrings, and core muscles. They help improve hip strength, posture, and athletic power—especially in movements like running, jumping, squatting, and lifting. This exercise is great for shaping and strengthening the lower body and can be done using just your body weight or with added resistance like a barbell or dumbbell.

How to do a basic hip thrust:

- Sit on the floor with your upper back resting against a bench or sturdy surface.
- Bend your knees and place your feet flat on the ground, hip-width apart.
- Roll a barbell or place a dumbbell over your hips if using weight.

- Lean back so your shoulder blades are resting on the edge of the bench.
- Press through your heels and lift your hips up toward the ceiling.
- Squeeze your glutes at the top, keeping your body in a straight line from shoulders to knees.
- Lower your hips back down with control, then repeat.
- Keep your chin slightly tucked and your core engaged to avoid arching your lower back. Make sure your feet stay flat and your knees don't cave in or fall outward.

Hip thrusts are one of the best exercises for glute development and lower-body strength. They're beginner-friendly, easy to progress, and make a great addition to any leg or full-body workout routine.

Calf Raises

Calf raises are a simple but effective exercise that targets the calf muscles at the back of your lower legs. They help improve ankle stability, balance, and overall leg strength. Strong calves support walking, running, jumping, and other daily movements, making this a great exercise for both beginners and experienced lifters.

How to do a basic standing calf raise:

- Stand with your feet hip-width apart and your toes pointing forward.
- Keep your legs straight but not locked and your hands by your sides or resting on a wall or chair for balance.
- Slowly rise up onto the balls of your feet, lifting your heels as high as you can.
- Pause at the top and squeeze your calf muscles.
- Lower your heels back down to the floor with control.
- Repeat for the desired number of reps.

To make the exercise harder, you can hold dumbbells in your hands or perform the move one leg at a time. You can also stand on a step or platform to allow a greater range of motion, letting your heels drop slightly below the level of your toes.

Calf raises are easy to add to any workout routine. They help build strength and endurance in your lower legs, which can protect you from injuries and improve performance in sports and daily activities.

Lat Pulldowns

Lat pulldowns are a machine-based exercise that mainly targets the latissimus dorsi muscles, which are the large muscles in your back. This exercise also works your biceps, shoulders, and upper back. Lat pulldowns help improve posture, back strength, and pulling power, making them a great choice for beginners and experienced lifters alike.

How to do a basic lat pulldown:

- Sit at the lat pulldown machine and adjust the thigh pad so your legs stay in place.
- Reach up and grab the bar with both hands, wider than shoulder-width, palms facing away from you.
- Sit tall with your chest up and your core engaged.
- Pull the bar down toward your upper chest by squeezing your shoulder blades together and bending your elbows.
- Keep your back straight and avoid leaning too far back.
- Pause briefly at the bottom of the movement.
- Slowly return the bar to the starting position with control.
- Repeat for the desired number of reps.

Start with a light weight to learn good form and gradually increase as you get stronger. Don't use momentum or swing your body—let your muscles do the work.

Lat pulldowns are a great way to build a strong, toned back and are especially helpful if you're working up to doing full pull-ups. They fit well into any upper-body or full-body training routine.

Box Jumps

Box jumps are a high-intensity plyometric exercise that help develop explosive power, coordination, and strength in your legs. They mainly target the quadriceps, hamstrings, glutes, and calves, while also engaging your core for stability. Box jumps can improve athletic performance, agility, and balance and are commonly used in sports training and conditioning.

How to do a basic box jump:

- Stand in front of a sturdy box or platform, with your feet shoulder-width apart and your knees slightly bent.
- Bend your knees and lower your hips to prepare for the jump.
- Swing your arms back for momentum, then quickly explode upward, jumping onto the box.
- As you jump, bring your knees up and land softly on the box with both feet.

- Make sure to land with your knees slightly bent to absorb the impact and keep your body balanced.
- Stand tall once you're on the box and then carefully step down one foot at a time to return to the starting position.
- Repeat for the desired number of reps.
- Start with a low box or platform to get the hang of the movement before progressing to higher boxes. Focus on controlled, powerful jumps rather than height alone.

Box jumps are excellent for improving your explosive leg strength and overall athletic ability. They also boost heart rate and help with agility and coordination.

Medicine Ball Slams

Medicine ball slams are a dynamic, full-body exercise that help improve strength, power, and cardiovascular endurance. They primarily target your core, shoulders, and arms, while also engaging your legs and back. This explosive movement is great for releasing stress and building functional power that can improve sports performance and overall fitness.

How to do a basic medicine ball slam:

- Stand with your feet shoulder-width apart and hold a medicine ball with both hands in front of you.
- Raise the ball overhead, keeping your core tight and your back straight.
- Engage your core and slam the ball down toward the ground as hard as you can, bending at the hips and knees slightly as you do.
- As the ball hits the ground, squat down and catch it with both hands to prepare for the next slam.
- Stand back up, bringing the ball overhead again, and repeat the motion.

Focus on using your whole body to generate power from the hips, not just your arms. The goal is to create a strong, explosive movement while maintaining control throughout the exercise.

Medicine ball slams are not only great for building strength but also for improving endurance and burning calories. They can be incorporated into high-intensity interval training (HIIT) routines or as a powerful addition to your core and full-body workouts.

Battle Ropes

Battle ropes are an excellent exercise for building strength, endurance, and power. They target your arms, shoulders, core, and even your legs, while also boosting cardiovascular fitness. This full-body workout is intense and dynamic, offering both strength and cardio benefits in one exercise.

How to do a basic battle rope wave:

- Start by standing with your feet shoulder-width apart, knees slightly bent, and your core engaged.
- Hold one end of the rope in each hand, with your arms straight and the ropes lying on the ground.
- With a firm grip on the ropes, quickly move your arms up and down to create waves in the ropes.
- Alternate your arms, making fast, controlled waves as high and deep as you can.
- Continue for a set amount of time (e.g., 30 seconds to 1 minute), then rest.

As you get more comfortable with the movement, you can increase the intensity by using heavier ropes, creating larger waves, or trying different variations like double waves (both arms move together), slams (swinging the ropes overhead and slamming them to the ground), or spirals.

Battle ropes are a great way to improve upper-body strength, conditioning, and endurance. They also help develop explosive power and coordination while burning a lot of calories. You can use them for short bursts of high-intensity work in circuit training or as part of a full-body workout.

Treadmill Sprints

Treadmill sprints are an excellent way to improve cardiovascular fitness, increase stamina, and burn fat. This high-intensity exercise targets your legs, core, and cardiovascular system, helping you build speed and endurance. Sprints on the treadmill can be adjusted in terms of speed and incline, making them adaptable to different fitness levels and goals.

How to do treadmill sprints:

- Start by warming up for 5-10 minutes at a moderate pace on the treadmill to get your body ready for intense activity.
- Set the treadmill to a high speed (fast running pace) that you can sprint at, but be sure it's still manageable for you.
- Begin sprinting at this speed for 20-30 seconds, focusing on fast, powerful strides and engaging your core.
- After the sprint, reduce the speed to a slower pace (light jog or walk) for 1-2 minutes to recover.
- Repeat the sprint and recovery cycle for 20-30 minutes, depending on your fitness level.

You can adjust the intensity by increasing the speed or adding incline to make the sprints more challenging. For beginners, it's best to start with shorter sprint intervals and longer recovery periods, gradually building up as you get more comfortable.

Treadmill sprints are great for building speed, burning calories, and improving heart health. They can be incorporated into high-intensity interval training (HIIT) workouts, or used on their own as a quick, effective cardio session.

Cycling

Cycling is a fantastic cardiovascular exercise that improves endurance, leg strength, and overall fitness. It's easy on the joints and can be done indoors on a stationary bike or outdoors on a regular bicycle. Cycling helps strengthen the quads, hamstrings, glutes, and calves while also improving heart health and burning calories.

How to do basic cycling (on a stationary bike):

- Start by adjusting the seat and handlebars to a comfortable position. Your knees should have a slight bend when the pedals are at their lowest point.
- Begin pedaling at a moderate pace to warm up for 5-10 minutes.
- Gradually increase the intensity by increasing your speed or adjusting the resistance on the bike.
- Focus on smooth, consistent pedal strokes. Keep your core tight and your back straight while maintaining a steady rhythm.
- Continue cycling for 20-45 minutes, depending on your fitness goals and level.
- Slow down for a cool-down period by reducing speed or resistance for the last 5-10 minutes.

Outdoor cycling:

- Start by ensuring your bike is properly adjusted and the tires are inflated.
- Find a safe, flat route to begin, and start with a moderate pace to warm up.
- As you get comfortable, increase your speed or choose routes with slight inclines to challenge yourself.
- Always wear a helmet for safety, especially on busy roads.

Cycling is low-impact but highly effective for building strength and endurance. It's a great way to fit in a workout that can be both enjoyable and easy to maintain. Whether indoors or outdoors, cycling offers a full-body workout while improving cardiovascular health and overall fitness.

Rowing

Rowing is an excellent full-body workout that improves cardiovascular fitness, builds muscle strength, and boosts endurance. It targets multiple muscle groups, including the back, shoulders, arms, core, and legs, making it an efficient and effective exercise. Rowing can be done on a rowing machine or, for outdoor workouts, on the water in a boat.

How to do basic rowing on a rowing machine:

- Sit on the rowing machine with your feet securely strapped in and your knees bent.
- Hold the handle with both hands, keeping your arms extended and your back straight.
- Start with your knees bent, your body leaning slightly forward, and your core engaged.
- Begin by pushing through your legs (not your arms), straightening your legs and using the power from your legs to start the stroke.
- As your legs straighten, lean back slightly and pull the handle towards your chest with your arms, keeping your elbows close to your body.
- Reverse the motion by extending your arms, leaning forward at the hips, and bending your knees to return to the starting position.
- Maintain a smooth, fluid motion and focus on controlled breathing throughout the exercise.
- Repeat for a set time or distance, depending on your workout goals.
- For beginners, start with shorter sessions and slower speeds, gradually increasing intensity as you get more comfortable with the technique.

Rowing is a low-impact exercise that provides a great full-body workout, helping you build strength and endurance while being easy on your joints. It's a versatile exercise that can fit into any fitness routine, whether you're looking to improve cardiovascular health, build muscle, or burn calories.

Pilates Core Exercises

Pilates core exercises are designed to strengthen and stabilize the muscles of your core, which includes your abdominals, lower back, and pelvic floor. These exercises focus on controlled movements, flexibility, and balance, and they help improve posture, reduce the risk of injury, and enhance overall body strength.

How to do a basic Pilates core exercise:

- Lie flat on your back with your legs extended and your arms by your sides.
- Engage your core and raise your legs to a 45-degree angle (or keep them bent at the knees for beginners).

- Lift your head, neck, and shoulders off the mat while keeping your arms straight and parallel to the floor.
- Begin pumping your arms up and down (about 6 inches) while inhaling for 5 counts and exhaling for 5 counts.
- Repeat for a total of 100 arm pumps, keeping your core tight and your movements controlled.

How to do a basic Pilates exercise: The Single-Leg Stretch

- Start lying on your back with your knees bent and your feet flat on the floor.
- Bring both knees into your chest, and lift your head, neck, and shoulders off the mat.
- Extend your right leg straight out at a 45-degree angle, keeping your left knee bent.
- Hold your right leg with both hands (one hand on your shin and the other on your ankle).
- As you exhale, switch legs, pulling your left knee into your chest while extending your right leg straight out.
- Continue alternating legs in a controlled, slow motion.

Pilates core exercises can be done without any equipment, making them perfect for home workouts. By focusing on proper alignment and breathing, these exercises improve core strength, flexibility, and stability, while also helping with muscle tone and posture. Regularly practicing Pilates can lead to a more sculpted and functional core.

Yoga Poses for Strength

Yoga poses for strength focus on building both physical power and mental resilience. Many yoga poses engage multiple muscle groups at once, promoting endurance, stability, and flexibility while improving overall body strength. Here are a few effective yoga poses that target various muscle groups to help build strength:

How to do basic yoga poses for strength:

1. Downward-Facing Dog (Adho Mukha Svanasana):

- Start in a tabletop position on your hands and knees.
- Lift your hips up and back, straightening your legs as you press your heels toward the floor.
- Keep your hands shoulder-width apart and feet hip-width apart, with your fingers spread wide and your arms straight.
- Push your chest towards your thighs and engage your core, lifting your tailbone higher.
- Hold the pose and breathe deeply, feeling a stretch in your shoulders, hamstrings, and calves.

- This pose strengthens the arms, shoulders, core, and legs while also stretching the back and hamstrings.

2. Warrior II (Virabhadrasana II):

- Stand tall with your feet wide apart.
- Turn your right foot out 90 degrees and bend your right knee, keeping it aligned with your ankle.
- Extend your arms straight out to the sides, palms facing down.
- Keep your gaze over your right hand and your chest open.
- Hold the position while engaging your legs, glutes, and core, then switch to the other side.
- Warrior II strengthens the legs, glutes, core, and arms while improving balance and stability.

3. Plank Pose (Phalakasana):

- Start in a push-up position with your hands directly under your shoulders.
- Keep your body in a straight line from head to heels, engaging your core and glutes.
- Keep your neck neutral by looking straight down at the floor.
- Hold the position, making sure not to let your hips sag or rise.
- Plank pose strengthens the core, shoulders, arms, and legs, and is a great way to build overall stability.

4. Chair Pose (Utkatasana):

- Stand with your feet hip-width apart, arms by your sides.
- Bend your knees and lower your hips as if you were going to sit in an invisible chair.
- Raise your arms straight overhead, keeping your biceps close to your ears.
- Engage your core and hold the position, keeping your knees behind your toes.
- Chair pose works the thighs, glutes, and core, while also helping with endurance and balance.

5. Boat Pose (Navasana):

- Sit on the floor with your knees bent and feet flat on the ground.
- Lean back slightly and lift your feet off the ground, balancing on your sit bones.
- Extend your legs so your body forms a V-shape, keeping your back straight.
- Reach your arms forward, keeping your chest lifted and core engaged.
- Hold the position, feeling the strength in your core and hip flexors.
- Boat pose targets the core, hip flexors, and balance, while also improving posture.

6. Bridge Pose (Setu Bandhasana):

- Lie on your back with your knees bent and feet flat on the floor, hip-width apart.
- Press your feet into the floor and lift your hips up toward the ceiling, squeezing your glutes.
- Keep your arms by your sides with palms facing down, or interlace your fingers under your back.
- Hold the pose while engaging your core and glutes to maintain stability.
- Bridge pose strengthens the glutes, lower back, and core, while also opening the chest and hips.

These yoga poses for strength are not only great for building muscle but also for improving flexibility, balance, and mental focus. Incorporating them into your regular yoga practice will help build a solid foundation of strength and increase body awareness.

Stretching for Recovery

Stretching for recovery is essential for maintaining flexibility, reducing muscle soreness, and helping your body heal after a workout. Proper stretching can improve circulation, relieve tension, and prevent injuries. It's most effective when done after your workout, once your muscles are warm. Here are a few gentle stretches that help your body recover and promote flexibility:

How to do basic recovery stretches:

1. Standing Forward Fold (Uttanasana):

- Stand tall with your feet hip-width apart.
- Slowly hinge at your hips and reach your hands toward the floor.
- Keep your knees slightly bent if you feel tension in your hamstrings.
- Relax your neck and let your head hang down, feeling a stretch along your spine, hamstrings, and calves.
- Hold the position for 30 seconds to 1 minute, breathing deeply.
- This stretch helps release tension in the hamstrings, lower back, and calves.

2. Cat-Cow Stretch (Marjaryasana-Bitilasana):

- Start on your hands and knees in a tabletop position, with your wrists under your shoulders and knees under your hips.
- Inhale and arch your back, dropping your belly toward the floor and lifting your head and tailbone (cow pose).
- Exhale and round your back, tucking your chin toward your chest and drawing your belly button toward your spine (cat pose).

- Repeat the flow for 5-10 breaths, moving slowly and smoothly between the two positions.
- This stretch gently mobilizes the spine and helps release tension in the back and neck.

3. Child's Pose (Balasana):

- Start on your knees with your big toes touching and knees spread apart.
- Lower your hips toward your heels and stretch your arms forward on the floor, bringing your forehead to the mat.
- Focus on relaxing your neck and breathing deeply into your back.
- Hold the pose for 1-2 minutes, feeling the stretch along your back, hips, and shoulders.
- Child's pose is a relaxing stretch that gently stretches the back, hips, and arms, helping to relieve tension.

4. Seated Forward Fold (Paschimottanasana):

- Sit on the floor with your legs extended straight in front of you.
- Inhale and lengthen your spine.
- Exhale and slowly hinge forward from your hips, reaching for your feet or shins (keep your back flat as you fold forward).
- Hold for 30 seconds to 1 minute, feeling a stretch along your hamstrings, lower back, and calves.
- This stretch targets the hamstrings and lower back, helping to improve flexibility and release tension in the legs.

5. Pigeon Pose (Eka Pada Rajakapotasana):

- Start in a tabletop position, then bring one knee forward toward your hands and extend the opposite leg straight behind you.
- Lower your hips toward the floor, keeping your back leg extended and your chest open.
- Relax your torso forward over your bent leg, reaching your arms out in front of you.
- Hold for 1-2 minutes on each side to stretch your hips, glutes, and lower back.
- Pigeon pose deeply stretches the hips and glutes, areas that often get tight after intense workouts.

6. Quadriceps Stretch (Standing or Lying):

- Stand tall and grab your right ankle with your right hand, pulling your heel toward your glutes.
- Keep your knees close together and your chest lifted, holding onto something for balance if needed.
- Hold for 20-30 seconds, then switch legs.

- If lying down, bend one knee and hold your ankle to your glute with both hands, keeping your hips square.
- This stretch targets the quadriceps and hip flexors, helping to release tension in the front of the legs.

7. Shoulder Stretch (Across the Chest):

- Stand or sit with your back straight.
- Extend one arm straight in front of you, then bring it across your chest at shoulder height.
- Use your opposite hand to gently pull your arm toward your chest, feeling a stretch in the shoulder and upper back.
- Hold for 20-30 seconds on each side.
- This stretch helps release tension in the shoulders and upper back, areas that often tighten up during workouts.

8. Hip Flexor Stretch (Lunge Stretch):

- Start in a lunge position, with one foot forward and the other knee on the ground.
- Push your hips forward, feeling a stretch in the front of your hip and thigh.
- Keep your back straight and hold for 20-30 seconds on each side.
- This stretch targets the hip flexors, which can become tight from activities like running and sitting for long periods.

Stretching for recovery should be done slowly and gently, without bouncing or forcing your body into a deeper stretch. Hold each stretch for 20-60 seconds, breathing deeply and focusing on relaxing your muscles. Incorporating these stretches into your post-workout routine will help you recover faster, prevent stiffness, and improve your flexibility over time.

Foam Rolling Techniques

Foam rolling is a self-myofascial release technique that helps relieve muscle tightness, improve blood flow, and increase flexibility. It's often used for muscle recovery, reducing soreness, and enhancing mobility.

How to foam roll:

- **Choose a foam roller:** Use a smooth or textured roller depending on the level of pressure you need.
- **Target muscle groups:** Roll slowly over muscles like your calves, quads, hamstrings, back, and glutes.
- **Apply pressure:** Position the foam roller under the muscle and use your body weight to apply pressure. Move slowly, pausing on tight or sore spots for 20-30 seconds.

- **Roll back and forth:** Gently roll back and forth, focusing on areas that feel tight. Avoid rolling directly over joints or bones.
- **Breath and relax:** Focus on deep breathing to help your muscles release tension as you roll.

Foam rolling after workouts can help reduce muscle stiffness and improve recovery. Start with gentle pressure and gradually increase as your body gets used to the technique.

CHAPTER 17

Your 20-Day Strength Training Journal

Tracking your progress is one of the best ways to stay motivated and make sure your efforts are leading you toward your goals. In this chapter, you'll find a 25-day strength training journal designed to help you log your workouts, monitor your performance, and track key factors like diet, sleep, and mood. By keeping a daily record, you can observe patterns, make informed adjustments to your routine, and celebrate your progress. Whether you're just getting started or you're a seasoned lifter, this journal will help you stay focused and accountable as you work toward becoming stronger and more confident.

How to Use This Journal

Each day's entry includes spaces for:

- **Workout Details:** Record the type of workout (e.g., full-body, push/pull, legs), exercises performed, sets, reps, and weights used.
- **Duration & Intensity:** Note how long you worked out and how intense the session felt (scale of 1–10).
- **Mood & Energy:** Track your emotional and physical state before and after training.
- **Sleep & Nutrition:** Write down how many hours you slept and any key notes on your meals, especially protein intake and hydration.
- **Notes & Adjustments:** Reflect on what went well, what could be improved, and any changes you plan to make.

Tip: Be consistent and honest with your entries. Even a "bad" workout day gives you valuable insight into your progress and helps you stay on track.

Use this journal daily, ideally filling it in right after your workout while your memory is fresh. Over time, you'll see trends that show what's working best for your body — and that's where real growth happens.

Day	Exercise	Diet	Mood	Sleep
1				
2				
3				
4				
5				
6				
7				
8				
9				
10				
11				
12				
13				
14				
15				
16				
17				
18				
19				
20				

CHAPTER 18

Yoga and Pilates for Strength Trainers

Incorporating yoga and Pilates into your strength training routine can significantly enhance your flexibility, balance, and core strength. These practices offer a deeper connection to your body, helping you improve posture, reduce the risk of injury, and recover faster. In this chapter, we'll explore how yoga and Pilates can complement your strength workouts by focusing on stability, mobility, and mindfulness. Whether you want to increase flexibility or build a solid foundation of core strength, integrating these practices can take your fitness to the next level and support your overall well-being.

Complementing strength with yoga

Complementing strength training with yoga can be highly beneficial for building a well-rounded fitness routine. While strength training focuses on building muscle, yoga enhances flexibility, mobility, and mental focus. Combining both can help you move more efficiently, recover faster, and improve your athletic performance.

Yoga promotes balance and stability, helping you perform strength exercises with better form and control. It stretches and lengthens muscles that may become tight from lifting, reducing the risk of injury and improving your range of motion. For example, after a lower-body strength session, yoga poses like Downward Dog and Pigeon can release tight hips and hamstrings, allowing your body to recover more effectively.

Additionally, yoga helps calm the nervous system and reduces stress, essential for recovery and mental well-being. Incorporating yoga into your weekly routine can boost your strength training progress by allowing your muscles to stay flexible, your mind to stay focused, and your body to remain in balance.

Whether you do an entire yoga session after strength training or incorporate a few yoga poses into your warm-up or cool-down, the benefits will support your overall fitness and help you maintain a healthy, strong body.

Key pilates exercises for core stability

Key Pilates exercises for core stability focus on strengthening the deep abdominal muscles, the obliques, and the lower back and pelvis muscles. These exercises promote better posture, support spinal alignment, and improve balance. Pilates is about controlled movements, so engaging your core throughout each exercise is essential. Here are some key Pilates exercises that will help build core stability:

1. The Plank:

- Start in a push-up position with your arms straight and shoulders aligned with your wrists.
- Keep your body straight from head to heels, engaging your core and keeping your hips level.
- Hold this position, focusing on maintaining a firm core. You can modify it by going onto your forearms if needed.
- This exercise targets the entire core and helps build stability.

2. The Hundred:

- Lie on your back with your knees bent and feet flat on the floor.
- Lift your legs to a tabletop position and curl your head, neck, and shoulders off the mat.
- Extend your arms by your sides and pump them up and down while taking deep breaths.
- Keep your core engaged throughout, focusing on controlled breathing and maintaining a strong, stable core.
- The Hundred works your abdominals and improves endurance.

3. Single-Leg Stretch:

- Lie on your back with your knees bent and your head and shoulders lifted off the mat.
- Extend one leg out while pulling the opposite knee toward your chest.
- Switch legs, alternating smoothly, and keep your core engaged while keeping your pelvis stable.
- This exercise targets the lower abs and works on coordination while maintaining stability.

4. Pilates Roll-Up:

- Start lying on your back with your arms extended overhead and legs straight.
- Slowly roll your body up one vertebra at a time, reaching toward your toes and engaging your core.
- Roll back down with control, using your core muscles to guide the movement.
- The Roll-Up targets the upper and lower abdominals, promoting spinal mobility and core control.

5. Leg Circles:

- Lie on your back with one leg extended toward the ceiling and the other flat on the mat.
- Draw small circles in the air with your extended leg, keeping your pelvis stable and core engaged.
- Reverse the direction of the circles after a few repetitions.
- This exercise works the lower abs and hip flexors while helping to improve pelvic stability.

6. The Saw:

- Sit with your legs extended wide apart and your arms stretched to the sides at shoulder height.
- Twist your torso to one side and reach your opposite hand toward the little toe of the opposite leg.
- Return to center and repeat on the other side, keeping your core engaged and your movements controlled.
- The Saw works the obliques and helps with spinal rotation and stability.

These Pilates exercises are excellent for strengthening the deep muscles of the core, improving balance, and promoting better overall posture. When practiced regularly, they will significantly enhance core stability, supporting your strength training efforts and helping to prevent injuries.

Integrating flexibility and strength

Integrating flexibility and strength into your workout routine is key to building a well-rounded fitness regimen. While strength training focuses on muscle building, flexibility exercises improve the range of motion, mobility, and recovery. Combining both elements allows for better performance, reduces the risk of injury, and helps maintain balance in your body.

When strength and flexibility are integrated, the muscles work more efficiently, and you can push harder during strength training without compromising your range of motion. For example, tight chest, shoulders, or hip muscles can limit your ability to perform exercises like squats or overhead presses with proper form. Stretching and flexibility work can help release tightness in those areas, improving your ability to move freely and with less strain.

A good way to integrate flexibility with strength is by incorporating dynamic stretches and mobility exercises into your warm-up before strength training. These help activate your muscles and improve their elasticity. Strength training, including static stretches or yoga poses during your cool-down, can help lengthen and relax the muscles you've worked, aiding recovery and reducing muscle soreness.

Adding Pilates and yoga to your routine is also a great way to integrate flexibility and strength. Pilates focuses on controlled movements that strengthen the core while improving flexibility, while yoga incorporates both strength and deep stretching, promoting overall balance and mental focus.

Balancing flexibility and strength will create a more balanced and functional body that performs better during workouts and feels better in daily life. Stretching can aid in recovery, improve posture, and enhance athletic performance, while strength training will give your muscles the power and endurance to support those movements. Together, they provide a strong foundation for overall fitness and long-term health.

Breathing techniques for performance enhancement

Breathing techniques for performance enhancement are essential for improving endurance, strength, and overall workout effectiveness. Proper breathing ensures your muscles receive enough oxygen and helps you stay focused, calm, and energized throughout your exercise routine. Whether lifting weights, running, or doing high-intensity workouts, mastering breath control can help you perform better and recover faster.

One common and effective technique is **diaphragmatic breathing** or **belly breathing**. This method involves deep breathing into the diaphragm rather than shallow chest breathing. By focusing on inflating your belly as you inhale, you engage your diaphragm fully, allowing for more air to reach your lungs and improving oxygen delivery to your muscles. Diaphragmatic breathing helps stabilize the core and reduces the risk of injury during squats or deadlifts.

Another helpful technique is **exhaling on exertion**. This technique helps you engage your core during strength training or other resistance exercises. For example, when performing a bicep curl, you would exhale as you lift the weight and inhale as you lower it back down. Exhaling during the exertion phase increases core stability and allows you to exert more force, improving the effectiveness of your movement.

Rhythmic breathing is a powerful strategy for endurance activities like running or cycling. By matching your breath to your movement, you can prevent fatigue and maintain a steady rhythm. For example, a 3:2 breathing ratio—where you inhale for three steps and exhale for two steps—helps runners maintain an efficient oxygen flow, ensuring your muscles don't tire too quickly. This pattern can also be adapted to fit your pace and energy levels.

Box breathing is another excellent technique, especially for high-intensity workouts. Box breathing involves inhaling for a count of four, holding your breath for four, exhaling for four, and holding again for four. This controlled breathing pattern improves oxygen intake and calms the nervous system, helping you stay focused and relaxed during stressful moments, like pushing through an intense interval or lifting a heavy weight.

Pursed-lip breathing is effective for controlling your breath during aerobic activities. You can manage airflow and prevent hyperventilation by inhaling deeply through the nose and exhaling slowly through pursed lips. This technique helps maintain steady energy levels and prevents you from feeling winded during long runs or cycling sessions.

Integrating these breathing techniques into your workout routine will improve your oxygenation, increase your strength, and improve your endurance. Consistent practice of proper breathing can help you push through fatigue, recover faster, and optimize your performance across all types of exercise.

CHAPTER 19

Overcoming Mental Barriers in Strength Training

Strength training is as much a mental challenge as a physical one. Overcoming mental barriers is crucial for progress, consistency, and achieving your fitness goals. This chapter delves into the common psychological hurdles many face in their strength training journey, such as fear of failure, lack of motivation, intimidation by the gym environment, and the frustration of plateaus. We'll explore practical strategies and techniques to break through these mental blocks, build a resilient mindset, and harness the power of positive thinking to enhance your training experience. Whether you are a beginner or a seasoned athlete, learning to navigate these mental challenges will empower you to push your limits, maintain focus, and succeed tremendously in your strength training endeavors.

Recognizing mental blocks

Recognizing mental blocks in strength training is crucial for progressing and enjoying your workouts. These blocks can appear in various ways and significantly affect how you approach your fitness goals.

One standard mental block is the fear of injury, which might come from past experiences or worries about the physical demands of lifting weights. This fear can lead you to avoid specific exercises or not to push yourself to lift heavier, even though you are capable.

Another block is a lack of confidence, which might make you feel like you don't belong in the gym or doubt your abilities. This often comes from comparing yourself to others or focusing on what you see as shortcomings rather than acknowledging your achievements.

Perfectionism can also be a mental block. If you set unrealistic standards for every workout, you might feel disappointed and discouraged if every session isn't at maximum intensity or if you don't see constant improvements.

Another significant hurdle is the fear of failure. Worrying that you won't reach your goals or will disappoint yourself or others can stop you from challenging yourself or setting ambitious goals.

Frustration from hitting a plateau is also common. Not seeing progress for an extended period can make you feel stuck and lose motivation.

Burnout from overtraining or insufficient rest can make you feel exhausted and disinterested in continuing your training routine.

Recognizing these mental blocks involves paying close attention to your thoughts and emotions related to your workouts. Are you skipping specific exercises out of fear? Do you feel upset if you don't perform perfectly every time? Understanding how your thoughts influence your actions in the gym is the first step in addressing and overcoming these blocks, helping you to engage more productively with your fitness regime.

Techniques for mental toughness

Building mental toughness is crucial for overcoming challenges in strength training and everyday life. A mentally tough mindset helps you push through tough times, handle stress better, and achieve your fitness goals. Here are some simple techniques to help you cultivate mental toughness:

Start by setting clear, achievable goals that challenge you but are still within your reach. Break these goals down into smaller, manageable tasks so you can celebrate small victories along the way. This approach helps build confidence and keeps your motivation high.

Consistency is another key element. Try to stick to your training schedule even when you're not feeling 100%. It's about creating discipline and a routine reinforcing your commitment to your goals.

The way you talk to yourself also influences your mindset and performance. Practice positive self-talk by replacing negative thoughts with positive affirmations. Instead of thinking, "I can't do this," tell yourself, "I'm improving with every session." Positive self-talk can significantly boost your confidence and reduce anxiety.

Spend a few minutes each day visualizing yourself achieving your goals. Imagine the process and the outcome in detail—completing a challenging workout, lifting a new personal best, or simply feeling strong and healthy. Visualization is a powerful tool that aligns your energy with your goals.

Learn to recognize when you're stressed and find effective ways to manage it. Techniques like deep breathing, meditation, or yoga can help reduce stress and improve overall mental resilience.

After each workout, reflect on what went well and what could be improved. Learning from each session helps you adjust your approach and better prepare for future challenges.

Don't underestimate the power of a supportive community. Surround yourself with people who encourage and motivate you. Whether it's a coach, a training partner, or a fitness community, having support can boost your morale and help you stay committed.

Building mental toughness takes time and practice, but by incorporating these strategies into your routine, you'll find that you're stronger physically, more resilient, and more confident in handling challenges.

Building a support system

Building a support system is essential for achieving and maintaining your strength training and overall fitness goals. A sound support system provides encouragement, advice, motivation, and accountability, helping you push through tough workouts and stick with your training plan even when challenges arise.

One effective way to build a support system is by joining a fitness community, such as a local gym, a fitness class, or an online group. Being around like-minded individuals with similar goals can motivate you and offer new strategies when facing plateaus. These communities also allow learning from others' experiences, which can keep your workouts engaging and effective.

Finding a workout partner is another excellent strategy. This could be a friend, family member, or coworker who shares your interest in fitness. Having someone to work with makes exercising more enjoyable and ensures you're less likely to skip a session. A partner can challenge you to push harder and help you stay committed to your routine.

Consider hiring a personal trainer if you're looking for professional guidance. A trainer can help you set realistic goals, customize your training plan, and navigate any barriers you encounter. They provide not only expertise but also personal attention and accountability.

Don't overlook the support that can come from family and friends who aren't necessarily joining you at the gym. They can encourage your efforts, celebrate your achievements, and understand your dietary and schedule needs, which is incredibly motivating.

Social media platforms and fitness apps are excellent for connecting with a broader community. Sharing your fitness journey online can inspire others and give you a sense of accountability. It's also a great way to receive feedback and support from people who are on similar paths.

Participating in competitions or joining community sports leagues can also enhance your motivation. These activities connect you with people who have similar interests and provide a competitive but supportive environment that can drive you to achieve more.

A strong support system transforms your training experience by preventing feelings of isolation, making workouts more enjoyable, and reinforcing your commitment to your fitness goals. Whether through community connections, professional guidance, or support from loved ones, building a network of encouragement and accountability can lead to significant progress and make your fitness journey a more holistic form of self-care.

Celebrating small wins and maintaining motivation

Celebrating small wins and maintaining motivation are critical components of a successful fitness journey. Often, the focus is placed on significant milestones, but recognizing and appreciating minor achievements can be just as crucial for keeping your spirits high and your dedication strong.

When you celebrate small victories, you create positive reinforcement that enhances your motivation and self-confidence. This could be as simple as acknowledging a week where you didn't miss a workout, recognizing improvements in your form, or noting that you've increased your endurance or strength, even slightly. Each of these achievements is a building block towards your larger goals.

Setting mini-goals along the way is helpful for effectively celebrating small wins. For example, you might aim to increase your weight lifting by five pounds or extend your cardio session by a few minutes. Achieving these smaller goals provides regular opportunities for celebration, keeping your enthusiasm and commitment alive.

Maintaining motivation can sometimes be challenging, especially when progress seems slow. One strategy to combat this is keeping a fitness journal. Writing down your workouts, how you felt, and what you accomplished tracks your progress and highlights how far you've come over time. On days when motivation wanes, looking back at your journal can provide a significant boost.

Another way to stay motivated is to vary your routine. Monotony can lead to boredom, which is often why people fall off their fitness regimen. By trying new exercises, changing your workout environment, or even switching the time of day you exercise, you can keep the experience fresh and engaging.

It's also beneficial to share your goals and progress with others, whether with a workout buddy, a coach, or an online community. This creates a support network that holds you accountable and celebrates your wins with you, making the journey more enjoyable and less isolated.

Remember, every step forward, no matter how small, is progress. By celebrating these moments and maintaining motivation through thoughtful strategies, you build a foundation of favorable habits and attitudes that benefit your physical health and enhance your overall life satisfaction.